T0147173

Rounding Third and Headed for Home

Memories and Reflections

John M. Rozeboom

WESTBOW
P R E S S®
A DIVISION OF THOMAS NELSON
& ZONDERVAN

WestBow Press books may be ordered through booksellers or by contacting:

WestBow Press
A Division of Thomas Nelson & Zondervan
1663 Liberty Drive
Bloomington, IN 47403
www.westbowpress.com
1 (866) 928-1240

Scripture taken from the King James Version of the Bible.

Address all correspondence to John M. Rozeboom
at 911 Garden Dr., Lynden, WA 98264 or email: rozeboomj@comcast.net

ISBN: 978-1-9736-7589-1 (sc)
ISBN: 978-1-9736-7588-4 (e)

Print information available on the last page.

WestBow Press rev. date: 10/14/2019

Contents

Forewords

It's a pleasure to write a foreword for this book of John M. Rozeboom. John M. and I (John A.) Rozeboom share as a grandfather - John Rozeboom. Reading these engaging vignettes from John's life, one's mind is quickly drawn to three sturdy foundations of a fruitful life – faith, family, and fun. John's narratives reeled me in from the start, not just because we are family. Many readers will find themselves in these stories.

Active, lived faith in Jesus Christ shines everywhere: what it is, how it acts. This book is about doing well in family life, playing ball, teaching, serving in ministry, coaching, and about doing lasting good. This book will stir up your faith.

I naturally latched on to John M. Rozeboom's family stories. For example, personal to us cousins but so interesting, stories about the six Rozeboom brothers, our dads and uncles. Except for John M's dad George and my dad Bill, they spent their whole lives around Edgerton, Minnesota. Good looking, dark-haired men of outgoing, sometimes boisterous demeanor, these guys loved us from our earliest years, taught hard work habits, and were so much fun to be around.

There is a lot of fun in this book, except it's called sport. John played many seasons of baseball in his life, coached year in and year out (taught English courses at the same time), worked hard at his craft, and became a member of the Washington High School Baseball Coaches' Hall of Fame. But the fun comes through. If you love baseball as I do, you will love the baseball in this book.

I like the image Daniel VanderKooi shared in his foreword picturing the reticence of a young JV player coming up the first time to practice on "the big varsity diamond." Ninety-foot baselines! I identify. Formidable, challenging like life. John M. Rozeboom, my cousin and life friend, has taught, cajoled, and showed hundreds of young men how to play the game and run the ninety-foot bases, successfully coaching baseball and lives.

-John A. Rozeboom, a pastor who also
loved the great game of baseball

A new way of living has crept up on us. We raise children at a breakneck pace, constantly looking for ways to entertain them. Too often we force them to play every possible sport in multiple leagues with coaches who are consumed with winning, often because of the pressure put on them by parents with unrealistic expectations for their children. It is not the children who choose this way of growing up. Rather it is the parents who have chosen to raise their children in the company of multiple youth sport coaches and in the company of their peers.

We need to slow down and re-think what is really important in life. Do we get children involved in athletics so they can hang out with their friends? Do we try to create superstars as a means of putting feathers in our own caps? Or are we too busy to make time to shoot a basket, play catch, or kick a ball with our children? By not taking the time, we miss out on many of the best parenting opportunities available.

Reading Coach Rozeboom's reflections on his coaching career should remind us all of the real value of sports. His reflections should cause us to reflect. By doing so, it is easy to fondly remember the many fun stories and youthful situations we experienced. Coach also does a great job of reliving games, stories, and teammates you may not have thought about in years. With Coach Rozeboom you are also guaranteed to recall everyone's nicknames and pertinent statistics.

As you read these reflections, you should think of many more personal experiences and names other than those shared by Coach Rozeboom. As you reflect on his reflections, think about the things that made your athletic experiences valuable. I think you will find relationships with teammates more valuable than statistics, trophies, or wins. I believe recalling the hard work, discipline, and life lessons taught by coaches like John Rozeboom will show you the real value of sport. Coach Rozeboom also shares many successes in a variety of walks of life that got their roots in the relationships, instruction, good times, and tough times of sport. Therein lives the beauty of athletics.

-Bill Blacquiere, a versatile athlete at and 1974 graduate of SCHS and a career educator and football coach

There are only a few people in my life to whom I don't refer to with their given names. Mom, Dad, Grandma, and Grampa, ... and Coach. The dictionary defines the word "coach" as someone who instructs. My definition of the word "coach" is John Rozeboom.

I have known Coach since April of 1996. That is when he had all of us Lynden Christian Jr. High baseball players come up to the big varsity diamond at the high school and take pre-game practice with the varsity. As a 13-year old baseball player I remember thinking this was pretty cool to share 3B with high school juniors and seniors.

My relationship with Coach started out from a distance. But soon I saw the many hours he would put into care of the field, his practice planning, and his classroom. As I moved into my sophomore year of high school, I became a regular player on the varsity under his leadership. I've always been a pretty laidback person, sometimes to a fault. This was the first time I really learned about time management. Coach would plan our practices down to the minute. I'm not talking about finishing a drill at 4:30 or practice getting done at 5:30. I am talking about fielding done at 4:17, a two-minute break for water and hitting practice starting at 4:19. What I didn't realize then was this attention to detail and the leadership that Coach displayed was helping to shape me and mold me for the rest of my life.

Fast forward 17 years and I am now privileged to hold a title that I sometimes feel inadequate to do … coach. I'll be entering my fifth year as the head baseball coach at LC and yet it feels like yesterday I was in the dugout with Coach Roze. The hard work and diligent effort he put into LC's program was just a glimpse into the man he was then and is today.

As you read through these memories of Coach's life you will realize how his work ethic and values were shaped - stories that are told in detail of days being raised out on the farm in the Sumas, WA area and the connection of family, friends, and trips back to Minnesota, and how a small rubber ball bouncing off of the side of an old barn turned into a passion for baseball and Coach's beloved Dodgers. These stories encompass his life, his passions, and his true love of Jeannie after over 50 years of marriage.

Often we are so wrapped up in the busyness of our lives we don't take time to pause and reflect on the journey our life has taken. People we are closest to us don't know much about us. The time and reflection that Coach has put into this has been incredible. I walked away feeling very blessed and humbled that I could be a small part of his life. I was such a small part to a man who played such a big role in mine. Way to go, Coach. You hit a homerun!

-Daniel Vander Kooi, a 2001 graduate of and now head baseball coach at LCHS and an insurance agent

Acknowledgements

Thank you to all who have contributed to this book's making.

Thank you to all my kin for their suggestions and help.

Thank you to many of my former students and ballplayers for their input.

Thank you to WestBow's graphic artist who has made the cover and back

Thank you to Cal Bratt and Henry Baron and my wife Jeannie for proofreading help.

Thank you to Jim VanderMay, John A. Rozeboom and Dave Schelhaas for their nudgings.

A Time Line

'42 Birth of John M. Rozeboom in Bellingham, WA and first home on the Ren DeBoer farm north of Lynden

'44 Move of the family to a farm near Sumas, WA

'48-'56 Schooling at Sumas Christian School with an 8th grade graduation

'57-'60 Schooling at Lynden Christian High School with a 12th grade graduation in '60

'61-'64 Schooling at Calvin College (now Calvin University) in Grand Rapids, MI with graduation in '64

'65 Marriage to Jeannie DeJong from Bellflower, CA

'65-'78 Birth of our three children and teaching years at South Christian High School in Grand Rapids

'78 Move of our family of five to a home in Lynden, WA

'78-'06 Teaching years at Lynden Christian High School in Lynden

'07 Wonderful retirement years with lots of volunteering

Preface

What prompted me to start writing this book was spending precious time with my 93-year-old dad George Rozeboom during 2009 in his latter days at the Christian Health Care Center in Lynden, WA and recording some of his life's stories. He valued the answer to Heidelberg Catechism's first question, "What Is Your only comfort in life and death?" He knew he "belonged." As I reached my 70's in birthdays, I began to think about our precious grandchildren and what they might know about the life of their Papa - me. I wanted Drew, Dani, Desi, and Dakota (of Dave and Deena), Liesl and Annemarie (of Paul and Sue), and Kenzie and Caden (of Josh and Kara) to know a little bit more about their Papa. When I talked to a friend, Dave Schelhaas from Iowa, after he had written his beautiful memoir about growing up in the town of Edgerton, he found his audience was much wider than just his heirs. In retrospect I can see how faith, family, and sports have richly impacted my life. After receiving my earliest draft of my journey, my cousin in Michigan urged me to share some of my sports' coaching stories. So that pursuit has led me into a lengthy last chapter. If nothing else, parts of my own life have been clarified to me in this writing process. Life is a gift, and there is a whole lot in the unwrapping.

Part 1

My Life Outside Coaching

Introduction

Who would've known the twists and turns of my life? When I was a little farm boy being raised near the foothills of the reigning Cascade Mountains a few miles south of Sumas, Washington, who could know what I would become after many things bigger than I and many personal choices that I would make in my life? I learned from Robert Frost's poem "The Road Not Taken" how "way leads on to way." I have concluded that my origin, path, and destiny were all determined before I was born, but I know that choices I have made have led to a variety of experiences and consequences. It's been a curious combo.

So now that I have passed three quarters of a century, it's high time for me to peek into the rearview mirror of my life. In baseball terms getting through high school was kind of like reaching first base, graduating from college was like getting to second base, and my lengthy teaching and coaching career of 42 years meant I had come to third base. I don't know how short or how long the last 90 feet will be, but I'm confident I am headed home. I have loved the great game of baseball, our national pastime, with a large crowd of memories that surround it. I guess I've become kind of a "diamond dear." But I also know there are things much bigger than baseball and sports. After reflecting on my life, I can clearly see that I've lived under a providential canopy by which God has richly blessed me in a variety of ways each step of the way.

1

A Country Boy

Where you come from makes a difference, actually many differences, in your life. My roots are in the country. During the depression era both my grandfathers were farmers; later so was my dad. My parents did not raise me in a little town like Lynden nor a big city like Grand Rapids or Seattle, but on a small country farm. I have learned how lack of space can produce problems. And I have learned a little about the space-affected problem of attention deficit disorder, and I have had minor issues myself with claustrophobia. But living in the country gave me lots of breathing room and a big sense of freedom as I grew.

In Ebenezer/DeBoer Hatchery country north of Lynden I spent my first three years. I followed the lead of the older neighborhood kids by tagging along after them on the adjoining Ren DeBoer and Ike Schouten farms; it seemed like I didn't have a care in the world. Just a week or two before my third birthday our family moved 10 miles to the East, to the Timmer farm that my folks first rented. Albert Timmer, Sr. was a crusty fellow with a hearty laugh and an ever-present pipe filled, of course, with Prince Albert tobacco. The 40-acre farm, just a mile east of Nooksack Valley High School and three miles south of Sumas, lay in front of the foothills of the beautiful Cascade Mountains. Upon the advice of his friend Joe Scheffer, Dad bought the farm after procuring a loan from another neighbor, Nick Honcoop, whom people thought was poor. Earlier the Bank of Sumas had denied Dad's attempt to get a loan there. Dad and Mom made that farm nestled by the foothills their own over nearly 40 years there. From a simple start many blessings have emerged.

Spring was a special season for the cows and me. The dairy cows, free from their stanchions and stalls of many months, frolicked in the pasture each springtime. Buds and blossoms were all over the place. Rejuvenation filled the air, and spring became my favorite season. Even the dandelions looked good to me then with the cows cavorting in the pasture. Eventually I celebrated each glorious and meaningful Easter. Naturally every spring also brought the fresh start for another season of building baseball hopes and relishing the sweet sound of the crack of the bat. Riding my horse or driving a tractor fast was also freeing. Dad, just like his dad, loved horses. Getting and riding my sorrel horse we named Kelly brought a nice diversion from farm work and my horn lessons. Getting on the 17-hands high horse did prove to be quite challenging. Not able to afford a saddle, I rode bareback, often with daring neighbor Gussy Buma on his spirited palomino and sometimes with Don Kamphouse on his horse in the foothills. Our family felt pretty private in our own yard except when we learned our neighbor lady Irene Buma had watched us through her binoculars until she complained that a corn crop was blocking her view.

Farm life at my folks' place was largely routine other than an every third year or so trip to Minnesota, where my folks were raised, and holiday gatherings with Mom's side of the family. As a young lad I began my day at 5:30 a.m. with my dad and a cup of tea in which I soaked graham crackers. Even at that early hour Dad readily noted and appreciated the beauty of the sunrise. The barn and chores beckoned. Dad's small herd of mostly Guernsey cows at first numbered only 23 in the mid-forties because the barn came with 23 stanchions till some later additions. The flat barn saw us feeding the cows, milking them with the De Laval machines, and cleaning up afterwards.

By 8:00 we were back in the house, and the oatmeal Dad

had started to simmer when he got up awaited us as a basic part of a hearty breakfast; Dad said the oatmeal stuck to your ribs. Regularly we ate it every Monday through Friday, but with yummy raisins on Saturdays; Corn Flakes on Sundays presented a very nice change-up. I grew up with the practice of the family altar. Each breakfast, lunch, and supper was begun with a prayer and ended with a passage of scripture. I think Dad read Ps. 42 most often; I can still hear "the waters roar" and the "be still" of Martin Luther's favorite psalm. After lunch at high noon Dad stretched out for a seven-minute nap in the living room till the ticker went off.

The flow of work stopped each day for the mid-morning coffee break and the mid-afternoon tea break accompanied by goodies. Supper at 5:15 meant we could be back in the barn to do the second milking between 6:00 and 7:30. Dad had to hustle with doing the chores to be on time for the many 8:00 board meetings that he attended. Beyond the routine the special seasons of haying and filling silo added work. Once after hearing about a bumper crop of an uncle in Minnesota, Dad and I found the height of a corn stalk at 13 feet. Dad made it clear that the seeds that he planted in the rich north Whatcom County soil turned into crops only with God's blessing. Doing a variety of kinds of jobs with the cows, calves, and chickens besides the seasonal field work taught me valuable lessons about responsibility. Dad, neither a task master nor a perfectionist, did expect his oldest son to be accountable for doing good work.

But Dad knew that all work and no play was no way to live a full day. We usually had some time to play and soak in the rich pleasures of country life. Mom's lush rose garden brightened our front yard. To the west of our house a 20-tree orchard abounded with sumptuous pears, plums, and all kinds of cherries and apples. When the cherries ripened and before the crows ate them, Dad would climb high in one tree and saw off a limb laden with sweetness for us kids. When my uncles, Lou and Elmer, from Minnesota came to visit one time, they paid the price after downing too many ripe plums. Sometimes I thought of the fruitful orchard on our farm as a second garden of Eden.

When I began my teaching career, I barely survived wearing a tie each day. Wearing a sport coat, shirt, and tie was required - that is, until one testing teacher, Mr. John VanderVeen, wore a turtleneck and that led to an altered dress code eventually for all the teachers. That occurred in the mid '60's. I felt hemmed in wearing a tie at school. Near the end of my teaching career getting out of my school clothes and hopping into my refereeing shirt and shorts to referee Middle School and junior varsity football games after school freed my spirit. Today I wear a tee shirt and shorts as often as possible all year long and anything like a hoody that goes over my head is a no-no; it's too confining. Working and playing in the country is a great way to live.

Owning a few acres with some horses and beef cattle along with a red barn and a white house is now a dream of the past for me. I don't miss some of the country smells that produced a distinctive dairy air; yet living in town I still miss the scent of fresh alfalfa and corn silage. The country offered open spaces with lots of room to roam, the lure of outside activities, and mountain majesty nearby. I was glad I was raised there. Many might say I was closer to a country hick than a city slick.

2

"Pumpkin" and Peace

During the December Japanese attack on Pearl Harbor I was residing in Mom's womb room. On 1-8-42 I arrived - in Bellingham, Washington at St. Luke's Hospital. My baby book says the hospital cost for the four days' stay totalled $28.05. At birth I weighed 8 ¾ lbs. with 21" of length. In a letter I received from my mom when I turned 22, she wrote about her first impressions of me, "You weren't a real pretty baby cuz you were bald and looked like a fat little prizefighter with your husky little arms and fists clenched up ready to go;" She added I was "sometimes restless but eager, obedient, and trusting." I shared my birth date with Elvis Presley, who was born 13 years earlier. A little research says Irving Berlin's "White Christmas" sung by Bing Crosby was a big 1942 hit. A new Ford auto cost $920, a gallon of gas 15 cents, and a gallon of milk 60 cents; the average income was $1,885. Franklin D. Roosevelt led the nation as the U.S. president, and the St. Louis Cardinals beat the New York Yankees in the 1942 World Series.

My first home was on the Ren DeBoer farm on the bend in the West Badger Road, a half mile west of the Guide Meridian and three miles north of Lynden. Rev. D. Hollebeek baptized me on 2-1-42 in the First Christian Reformed Church in Lynden. Later, I remember the consistory members filing in at the front of church and one of the elders, Clarence Vander Griend, often slipping me a peppermint. That always made church sweeter. The historic

DeBoer rental house where I first lived measured all of 300 square feet; that house became legendary as a starter home. My dad soon farmed in a 50/50 arrangement with Ren overseeing the chickens and my dad the cows.

At 9 ½ months I was walking. I was called "Pumpkin" and "Butterball" (I was pretty round as photos reveal) and later "Johnny." In contrast to the mound of stuffed animals along with his pet blanket and binky of my grandson "Dookie," I can only recall having one scrawny, well-worn little brown monkey that I cherished for nap times. My parents used Kathleen DeBoer, a daughter of Ren and Lena, as my babysitter; she later married Alvin Plantinga, who eventually became a very highly acclaimed expert as a philosophy professor. Denny, Ren's son, much later became a valued member of an early Tuesday morning Prayer and Share group I joined in the early '80's; at church on Sunday morning I cherished the warmth of frequent hugs from Betty, Denny's wonderful wife. Later I had the privilege of coaching Denny's son Roger in high school football and baseball. I had a very happy almost three years there, especially as a tagalong to the nearby neighborhood kids - the older Schouten kids and Maurice DeBoer, the youngest son of Ren and Lena. According to my mom's record, my first full sentence was, "Daddy read Bible." My sister Ida Ann was born in October just a couple months before our family's big move east. I had let my mom's pregnancy out of the bag to the DeBoers when I announced the "buggers under the bed" – a new baby buggy that awaited my sister's arrival. Rumor has it that I never cried in my nearly three years on that DeBoer farm. I did not choose my birthplace or my parents, but my early surroundings have profoundly influenced and blessed me. In addition, Dad and Mom came from some solid stock. It is a big bonus to be born into a good environment and receive good genes besides; the advantages are far reaching.

3

Dutch and Much Much More

The family into which I came loved me. It's quite a long tale. Whatever fame I can be associated with came long before me and can be found in a remote connection on my mom's side. Four generations back on my maternal side, Bastiaan DeKoekkoek (1835-1923=88) was my great great-grandfather, and he married Adriana DeGroot, a descendent of the honored-with-a-statue-in-Holland Hugo DeGroot (Grotius on the statue), a pioneer in international law in the early 17th century and also a Dutch statesman and scholar. Johannes Paulus DeKoekkoek (1859-1938=79), my great grandfather, was their son, and he married Elizabeth Mesman (1861-1949=80); they emigrated from Hillegom in the Netherlands and immigrated to America in 1907.

One of their 12 kids, my grandfather Gerard DeKoekkoek (1895-1984 =89), a dairyman, later married Ida Hanenburg (1899-1967=68), a strong minded and bustling lady, and they became the parents of my mother Elizabeth (1919-2007=87}, a very sensitive and artistic lady born on December 29, and her three siblings – Ted, Rachel, and Gerard, Jr. in Edgerton, Minnesota. Much later Ted married Jo VanderWerff in Seattle and lived there, Rachel married Howard VanAalsburg, and Gerard married Marion Baldwin, and both families lived in the Lynden area. I clearly remember the brother of my Gramma Ida DeKoekkoek, Rev. John Hanenburg, who had an imposing presence with his erect posture and big belly which jiggled during his infectious laughter; his daughter Irene married Dr. Stanley Wiersma, a prominent Calvin College professor for many years and my instructor in a 17th century English class. Getting a straight A on one major paper for Dr. Wiersma made my buttons pop; that high a grade was not so common for me.

Elizabeth ("Toots") married my father, George Rozeboom, in 1940 (December 27) on a farmyard near Ferndale, Washington. In 1971 widower Grampa DeKoekkoek (A koek is a cookie in Dutch) married Minnie Bajema. Paul (1890-1982=92), a brother of my grampa, became a vigorous preacher and missionary, especially in the Pacific Northwest; his end came when he died tragically in a house fire. Both Elizabeth and her father Gerard, Sr. died from congestive heart failure. I was born as the oldest grandchild on my mom's side. Mom's side enjoyed living but very seriously valued education and excellence. Mom's side brought me 14 cousins. Uncle Howard and uncle Ted served in our country's armed forces. Uncle Gerard went to serve but came home in one day; a hair over 6'6," he was deemed to be too tall.

On my paternal side my dad George (1916-2012=96) was born to my grandfather John Rozeboom (1891-1940=49) and his wife Anna Eekhof (1894-1993=99) in Kanahwa, Iowa. Like my maternal Grampa Gerard DeKoekKoek, Grampa John, a dairy farmer who also lost his Minnesota farm to a bank in the 1930's depression, had to start over. His life on earth ended when pneumonia set in after he broke his neck in a car accident which occurred as he was getting ice cream (no refrigeration then) to reward the hay helpers on his farm. His oldest son, my father George, left his six siblings - Josie, Bill, Elmer, Marv, Bud, and Vern, and other Minnesota kin in 1938 to follow his "Toots" to and work in Whatcom County of the Pacific Northwest; and that's where he lived for the rest of his life. Earlier my dad said he remembers being "distracted" in church by the long, blond curls of "Toots" when they both attended church in Edgerton. Later his siblings' marriage partners respectively were Lou Schaap, Leola Geerdes, Emma Mulder, Alma Bolt, Clara Kooiker, and Harriet DeBoer. Harriet, as a widow, later married

John VanderHaar, a very capable and kind man. My uncles Vern and Elmer died from lung cancer in their 60's after years of Lucky Strikes and Camel cigarettes (boy, could they blow smoke rings!) while Uncle Bud died at age 80, Uncle Bill at 92, and Aunt Josie at 99; a horse-shoe player of some fame, Uncle Marv is advancing in the 90's club, and at the latest count he has 46 great-grandchildren - 23 girls and 23 boys. I became the oldest grandchild on my father's side after Lee Ann, the oldest child of Aunt Josie and Uncle Lou Schaap, tragically died when she fell into a wash tub of lye and drowned at the age of three in 1940. Dad's side of the family clearly valued a love of life and laughter with a lot of generosity included. Dad's side brought me 21 cousins. I wish I could've met my Grampa John, but getting to know three of my four grandparents pretty well blessed me richly; it's something I cherish. I am proud of all my uncles who served in the U.S. military; this includes Uncle Bill and Uncle Vern on the Rozeboom side.

A third generation American and from Northern European (Dutch and German) stock, I am the grateful recipient of a rich spiritual heritage; virtually all my known forbears have drawn upon and lived by Christian faith. My four grandparents all came to the United States in the huge immigration explosion of the late 1800's and early 1900's. In that regard I am a very typical American. I am grateful for the apostle Paul's missionary journeys many centuries earlier as they led to a budding Christianity spreading into Spain and then blossoming into northern Europe, where my ancestors came from. I am richly blessed with the fruit of that inheritance that has led to my Christian faith which has served as an anchor in my life.

Although my identity as the heir of largely Dutch forefathers is not my whole story, it did land me in some rather Dutch-centered enclaves in Washington, Minnesota, and Michigan. And I have learned about the value of cleanliness, neatness, and orderliness from some staunch folks. My life has been built on a solid foundation of places, people, and principles. But mingling with a variety of folks beyond family has wonderfully broadened me. Now

I can comfortably engage people of various ethnic and religious backgrounds. For me eating more Italian food soon became an acquired taste ushered in by my first pizza in the late 1950's at Shakee's in Bellingham. I learned all the red stuff I poured over my Mexican food at the Fiesta Café with faculty friends in the mid-1960's in Grand Rapids was not ketchup. But every Christmas season I lick my lips over the tasty Dutch pastry treat – olie bollen.

I think Whatcom County where I was raised was about 95% white in the mid-20th century. Later playing basketball with a former world heavyweight champ, who was an Afro-American, helped to stretch me. Being in a Bible study with a variety of faith backgrounds during the '70's helped me to distinguish between majors and minors in my religious life. Together we learned to laugh at petty religious differences and rally around our relationships with Jesus, our Lord and Savior. My main identity, as a child of the King, is priceless for me in the present and for my long-term future. I am grateful for other acquired identities – a husband, a father, a papa, an uncle, a friend, an English teacher, a Third Church member, a neighbor, a summer house painter, a coach, a Rozeboom, a Lync, a Knight, a Sailor, a Michigander (for 18 years), a Washingtonian, an American, a fan of the Dodgers (and Mariners), Packers, and Lakers, a fan of the Huskies and Zags, a member of the Silent Generation (pre-the baby boomers of 1946 and later) and more.

4

Holidays

Holidays such as Memorial Day and the Fourth of July found the DeKoekkoek clan of my mom's side clustering and celebrating at choice scenic spots – Birch Bay, Mt. Baker, Nooksack Falls, Vancouver's Stanley Park with its zoo, Chilliwack's Cultus Lake, Berthusen Park just north of Lynden, the Peace Arch in Blaine, and Deception Pass near Oak Harbor. From ski to sea and between, all these places were inviting in different ways. I thoroughly enjoyed my mom's tasty potato salad, always the best of a grand array of food choices capped off by Gram DeKoekkoek's delicious pies. Thanksgiving at Grampa Dekoekkoek's farm on the Oatcole Road near Everson became a special annual treat with lots of delicious food and laughter; trying to play football with my cousins after consuming too many sumptuous deserts provided a hefty challenge for us kids. Being away from that nostalgic gathering time for my first Thanksgiving at college in Michigan was an acid test I had to pass. Holidays brought our extended family together in a warm way.

Mom also created festive birthday parties for us kids; capturing parts of these events on camera, a super-8 milli-meter, and with snapshots was a must for her! A lengthy tradition developed around our immediate family's celebration of my dad's birthday every June with a wiener roast by the swamp bridge at the south end of the farm. On one occasion our dog ate most of the buns so we had to eat bun-less dogs. June 6 has provided a lasting imprint on us kids' memories. No birthday in our family passed without cake and candles and a gift or two. I enjoyed all the celebrations.

5

Worlds of Imagination

Farming activities surrounded my young life, but in the midst of it all I exercised my imagination. At age five I received a long prized Christmas gift, a 2' high and 3' long hip-roofed red barn which my dad spent a lot of late evenings constructing; it led to hours of delightful play for this little farmer with his little cows, horses, and tractors. In my very free early grade school days I loved to "pretend farm." Imitating Shorty, a neighbor's hired man, I wore a straw hat and rolled up some paper for a cigarette as I gathered grass clippings along the road in my wagon to bring to my "silo," a 50-gallon drum. Often when Dad milked his cows, I "milked" my mine, 4' long and 4" wide boards with four appropriately placed nails for teats about 2/3's the way down; I leaned my "cows" against a wall so they could be properly washed, milked, and salved. For sister "Pooky" and two neighbor girls, Janet and Monie Bierlink about the same age, I served very cheerfully as a benevolent dictator orchestrating our child play. I guess my gifts of administration and organization were getting a start already as a youngster.

As a little chap I could see that Mom was fascinated with words. And her reading in our living room stirred my imagination. From the tearful story of <u>Beautiful Joe</u> that she read to me as I curled up next to her on the couch, I still can visualize that poor, abused dog with his ears chopped off by his merciless master, Mr. Jenkins. Over and over we read together <u>Black Beauty</u>, a majestic horse

15

story. Mom also helped me memorize, "The Lord is my shepherd; I shall not want" from Psalm 23: 1 (KJV) as well as some other psalms. Her reading times certainly spurred on my imagination and love of words.

In the barn I hung on every word of Dad's concocted stories that he shared with me while we were milking. But the stories of Sergeant Preston and his dog King sometimes interrupted the flow of my barn chores as I crowded by the barn radio to hear an exciting part of a story. In grade school I enjoyed reading about the pursuits of the Hardy boys and the Sugar Creek Gang. Toward the end of my grade school experience I checked out from the public library in Sumas and read a lot of rough, tough cowboy stories. These stories led to my own concoction of a gang led by Knife Gunnison; I pretended to be Knife as I carried my bb gun around the farm. I had drawn a picture of each bearded member of the gang.

My entry into the sports world occurred at age nine when I purchased my first baseball glove, a $3.95 Sears Roebuck "gem." Oh, the rich smell of its leather! Soon I was creating players for imaginary football, basketball, and baseball teams and games. Even to this day I recall the names of a couple of those players – quick little lefty Chuck Evans and big righty Buck Brill. In 1953 at age 11 I got my first package of baseball cards with some stiff pink bubble gum tucked inside. One of my first packs contained a card of the Brooklyn Dodgers' centerfielder Duke Snider (affectionately pronounced "Dook" in Brooklyn-ese as he was called the Duke of Flatbush, an area in Brooklyn by Ebbets Field, where he hit many of his 40 or more homers in five consecutive seasons). That started my long allegiance to the Dodgers and lots of games I concocted as I pretended to be Dodger players in games, or out on the tractor broadcasting an imaginary Dodger game while clipping thistles in the pasture. And since I have given all my eight grandchildren a pet name, five-year old Caden is now my "Dookie." How rich reading and playing was, is, and can be!

6

Fears

Having my bedroom door open as a youngster, I found comfort from the kitchen light that helped me go to sleep. For quite a while when I left the barn to go to the house, I raced; I felt like there might be a Boogie man lurking in the dark. As a kid I feared the dark. After the Russian dictator Nikita Khrushchev brazenly declared he'd bury America, Dad named one wagon that he didn't like "Krushev." Many Americans had some kind of fear of the "commies" in the 1950's, a time of some nasty witch hunts. My two dominant fears of my younger years were tied to the times. For one, I believed that I might be captured by the Communists, and with my tender neck placed over a block of wood, I'd be asked if I loved Jesus; if I said yes, a hatchet would separate my head from my body and I would die young. Or, if I lived longer, the army would draft me into serving for my country, and my life would quickly be over when a bullet in battle would send me into eternity.

Early on I learned to have a healthy respect for my parents and authority figures and God. At first it was close to fear. How does a child learn to obey where there are no clear limits? Spankings at home and at school when I was in grade school taught me some lessons. At home my dad didn't like it one bit when I was disrespectful to my mom and/or my sister. As a consequence I had a couple visits to the woodshed. When I became a dad, giving our kids a spanking gave me no joy. For me a spanking meant using an objective piece of wood, a wooden ladle, to apply smartly to the naughty child's hind end till a little later the sting and tears led to an apology for a wrong done. No doubt about it, parenting does take a lot of judgment and wisdom.

7

Accidents?

Mom used to share at breakfast from her dreams the night before some of the harrowing experiences that could possibly occur on the farm. It's led me to ponder often a couple of my experiences.

With Dad on the front of a hay wagon and ancient neighbor Archie Walker bucking 60-pound bales of local hay up to Dad, I was the six-year old "navigator" of Dad's sparkling red "C" Farmall tractor pulling the wagon. Two shirtless teenagers, riding at the back of a hay baler on which they tied the wires, attracted my attention; each time they made a smaller loop inside the field they'd give me a wave or gesture. Once when I was watching them, a hay bale sneaked up on me and I was vaulted from our tricycle type tractor into the air. I yet marvel how I missed the tractor's drawbar and wagon's tongue in my descent. I landed just inside the path of the tires of the hay wagon. Evidently Dad caught up with the driverless tractor and killed the motor before racing back in the field to find me still dazed and lying on the ground. My straw hat was up field where one of the wagon's tires had flattened it. I was only stunned. Dad leaned over me and said, "We're not telling Mom about this either." When I reflect on that accident now, I can see why I believe in guardian angels that overcome human carelessness. I did learn to be more aware when I was driving. Dad had to wait till the end of WWII to get that precious tractor off the assembly line. Dad had used a jitney, a shaved truck with no brakes as it served as a surrogate tractor for a couple years before the coveted tractor arrived in 1948.

Another incident occurred when we were putting hay in the barn. To unload the hay Dad would stand on the load and sink the four hay forks into a group of 12 bales at a time. A cable ran through the pulley. The cable would often kink above the pulley as it tightened from the hay load to the top of the barn and on the track near the ceiling of the hay mow on to the tractor-pulled cable at the other end of the barn. After the bales reached the haymow, Dad would pull the rope to release the bales. I was a 10-year old fourth grader when Dad got his fingers caught untwisting the cable and rode the 12 bales almost to the top of the barn before I could just see his plight from my view at the edge of the barn. Quickly I backed the tractor to the barn and Dad got his smashed fingers out of the pulley. I was quite indignant that Dad with a couple broken fingers wouldn't let me drive him in our '38 brown Chevy the three miles to see a doctor in Sumas; after all I had driven that manual shift car several times on the yard and in the pastures. I guess human error was involved again in this incident, but I'm thankful that the hurt to Dad was limited.

Two days before Christmas 2014 Jeannie and I avoided a head on car collision just north of Bellingham. In pretty heavy traffic and traveling at 45 miles per hour, Jeannie drove onto the shoulder of the Northwest Road after a car drifted toward us. The sleepy driver scraped the left side of the back of our car and shot us into a 180-degree turn and slide, where we amazingly avoided any of the two-way traffic. Our lives were spared and we were not injured, but "Queenie," our champagne-colored 2013 Chevy Equinox, took it pretty hard. After $10,000 in repairs and 10 weeks at the auto body shop, we got her back just in time for our trip to Arizona for spring training. A guardian angel had protected us again after another human error.

If God cares for every sparrow's needs and every hair on my head, I know He cares for all He has created. Accidents, such as collisions on the highway, usually occur because of one or more human errors. There are lots of opinions about good luck and bad luck. But I question whether luck exists. A bloop hit off a big righthand hitter's bat that touches the chalk down the right field line after a great pitch nearly eludes the batter may seem like luck. But is it? The pitcher fooled the batter only partially. In His grand design does God even care about a pitch or hit? It seems to me what we often describe as luck is an incomplete interpretation of what has happened. So where is luck or good breaks in a world run by a Providential God, who permits good and bad things to happen to good and bad people and who works in and through all things? Lots of bad experiences have produced a harvest of good in people's lives. Christians often like to thank a providential God just for good things that occur in their lives; they like to say, "That was a God thing." And doesn't good often come out of what seemed at first bad? Do we ask enough what are the miracles that happen every day? Each day I'm alive I've been given breath, and it is not my choice. I don't think I believe in fate or luck; that sounds like a universe not cared for by a sovereign God. I believe God does care about things big and small, but I don't know how; yet I know I'm more than a pawn in His hand. I don't believe things just happen. Certainly there is a lot of life I don't yet understand. But I hang my faith hat on the Romans passage (8:28 in NIV) that says, "In all things God works for the good of those who love Him."

8

Minnesota Tripping

Trips to Minnesota, about every three years, brought special times of getting acquainted with family, especially with the Rozeboom side of the family tree. Though once by Amtrak, we usually traveled by car for the 1700-mile trek "back east," as Dad described it. All my uncles there knew how to laugh and enjoy themselves; nobody seemed uptight. At age four or five riding Uncle Vernie's Shetland ponies thrilled me; Mom recorded it on her movie camera. Sometime later one of Uncle Vern's cigarettes became my first; the sneaky event occurred behind a corn crib. Wearing a clown's suit and letting off firecrackers while riding along with Uncle Elmer in his sports car down Edgerton's Main Street past the Leader Cafe in the Dutch Parade produced a noisy, but joyful highlight of another trip to Minnesota Twin's country.

A couple of cousins particularly stand out to me; John Arlyn ("Yun") of Uncle Bill, like me, was named after Grampa John. John A's hearty laughter has always been wonderful. Once his family visited us in Washington; building forts together in our dry swamp and hanging on cows' tails for a pasture thrill ride was a lot of fun. As an adult Yun became a wonderful pastor and then missionary overseer who impacted many. His younger brother Billy was special too: spiritually precocious, he was called a "blue baby;" he died in 1955 right after a heart valve repair surgery failed at Mayo Clinic. Dad picked me up from grade school that day and said flatly, "Billy died." Cousin Ron of Uncle Lou and Aunt Josie lived joyfully into his 50's as a robust fellow with Down Syndrome; he fervently protected his women relatives, and I remember he called the ducks on the Schaap farm "gucks." While most of my Minnesota uncles were farmers, Uncle Bill trucked gas to farmers and Uncle Elmer had quite an array of huge machinery for construction and snow removal. I truly relished my visits to the family farm east of town where the widowed Anna, my gramma, long lived, then Uncle Vern and Aunt Harriet farmed – raising hogs, and later cousin Lou Ann, of Uncle Lou, and her husband Gene Kuiper and family have lived.

Partly I was "schooled" by learning my first dirty jokes in a tree hut in Edgerton by an older, more worldly-wise Cliff Christians. It was up in that tree where I learned this nonsensical ditty: "I had a little monkey, I had a little monkey; I fed him gingerbread; I set him on the binder and shot him in the hinder, and now my little monkey is dead." I also still remember a joke about a rooster, chick, and donkey. Hunting gophers with "Yun" and bounding jack rabbits in huge fields with cousins Aud and John Fritz by the Schaap farm at night provided exciting ventures in those visits. A friend of Yun, Dave Schelhaas, would later become one of my college roommates in my junior year at Calvin after he moved on from Dordt's then two-year program. Earlier I certainly was envious of town kids when I watched Dave play summer legion baseball; at home I would have been milking cows during those game times. Separating from family always hurt. I remember tender uncle Bud had tears in his eyes as we had to leave Minnesota after one visit there in the late '40's. But seeing Mt. Rushmore and the reigning Rockies as well as visiting the famous Wall Drug in South Dakota created special memories on trips back to Washington. I really treasured my saddle-shaped ring purchased on one trip when we visited Wall Drug. Trips to the Midwest created many fond memories and gave me a sense of double belonging.

9

Church – Practices, Stats, and Priorities

After the move east near Sumas on the East Badger (earlier named the Schuette Road), our family began attending the Sumas Christian Reformed Church. At home before each meal we kids were taught to pray, "God bless this food and drink for Jesus' sake. Amen." Now two of our grandkids use these words before lunch, "Father, Father, once again, once again, thank you for our blessings, thank you for our blessings. Amen. Amen." Once visiting Minnesota cousins said their premeal prayer so fast we couldn't figure out the words. And before going to bed, we as kids prayed, "Now I lay me down to sleep; I pray the Lord my soul to keep, and if I die before I wake, I pray the Lord my soul to take." Later in life I learned I could pray using a variety of words at any time and any place.

My parents regularly took us kids to church with them on Sundays. Services were held at 10:00 in the morning and at 2:00 in the afternoon. During the second service some of the men in our farming community seemed to show their agreement with a sermon's point even if they didn't hear it exactly; after a week's work they were so tired they gave their nodding approvals. Counting tiles in the church's ceiling helped some to keep awake. Since I loved baseball, I dutifully added up all the numbers of the posted hymn numbers, usually four or five, and calculated in my head the average song number. I always hoped for high numbers, mostly in the 300's and 400's, because the average of those numbers I figured could be my batting average the next fastpitch or baseball season. I also could imagine the preacher as a pitcher on his mound and me as a batter ripping base-hits back past him. One message I do remember. Rev. Verwolf's sermon on "Dare to be a Daniel" impacted me – "Dare to have a purpose firm; dare to make it known." To say my spiritual priorities heading into high school were not always admirable is right, but I was given a solid foundation. I was set up for one big curve ball in high school, a wake up call.

10

Initiations and Rites of Passage

Looking back, I remember some hoops I had to jump through. I guess my one kindergarten day was a kind of initiation. Later, nearly getting "pantsed" by some bigger boys in a Pete Bosman bean patch was a narrow escape. I heard about a neighbor at Nooksack Valley High School who as a freshman had his underpants removed and then mounted on the flagpole, but for me the special freshman orientation was mighty mild. It required all of us "freshies" to push a peanut with our nose from one end of the basketball court to the other; Rhonda VanderPol crawled on the cold floor right next to me in that race.

Stories of what happened on the Sumas bus were legendary. Some of my experiences were not all that positive. I recall a troop of big senior guys ruling the bus when I rode it as a freshman. Dave Verwolf, Elton Visser, Alan "Arly Bug-up" Groen, Jay "Flea Hole" DeVries, and Herb "Pits" Advocaat as sometimes rather ruthless big boys sat near the back of the bus and exercised their power. The girls pretty much sat near the front of the bus. Through his coke bottom glasses the elderly bus driver, Ray Bajema, could not see what was happening behind him. Sometimes the big intimidators "farried" freshman boys; this meant one tormenter would twist the shirt of a "freshie" while pinching a little skin underneath it.

Sometimes the freshie's hair would get messed up. Sometimes a lunch was grabbed and parceled out by the seniors with words like, "Hey, Pits, you want a tasty chocolate chip cookie?" or "How about a fresh orange, Flea?" One time when I felt my frustration mounting and I thought I had been tortured enough, I took a swing at big Dave Verwolf; my punch to his arm just bounced harmlessly off. His return punch almost went through my upper arm; it felt like it came out in my armpit. I was humiliated that day. Later after watching how the big boys treated "Pits," I concluded the lanky, redheaded Canadian was their weak link. Weeks later he tried to harass me. I shocked him with a smack to his nose and heard the other seniors' responses, "What's the matter, Pits?" as they laughed at him. Thereafter I was no longer one of an endangered species. That was last time in my life that I remember seriously punching somebody. I was grateful that my tender mom once told me that fighting should be avoided if at all possible, but there may be a time when you have to stand up for yourself or another. Later the "Just War" theory originating from a defensive position for our nation to stop evil abroad made pretty good sense to me.

The hazing issue has raised its ugly head in more than one school or university or team. Having a hoop to jump through before joining a group or team or organization doesn't sound too threatening, but in some places the initiation rites have gone way too far and have produced horrible consequences. I appreciate all attempts to do justice as well as make peace.

11

Education for My Mom and Dad

Someone has defined the word education as "the leading out from ignorance." Getting more formal education should make a person humbler as each mountain of knowledge one masters leads to bigger worlds of knowledge beyond it. But sometimes getting even a little education leads sadly to arrogance in some people. It's hard to deny that experience is just about as important as book learning. Both are needed. The times in which people live often dictate what kind of opportunities for formal education exist. Though common sense really isn't so common, my parents seemed to have had a pretty good grip on it and an accompanying wisdom too.

In 1929 when the "roaring '20's" didn't seem to reach Edgerton and a lot of other places, my dad completed eight years at a country schoolhouse. I doubt that Dad ever heard about Babe Ruth or F. Scott Fitzgerald, who were making headlines on the east coast. Dad recalled the graduation treat for his country school class of three was seeing the movie of <u>Uncle Tom's Cabin</u> after reading Harriet Beecher Stowe's convicting novel; he often said he could hear in his mind's ear the bull whip's snap as the slaves were being lashed. Though Mom and her siblings finished the 12th grade, none of Dad's did. After her junior year Mom had to work a year before finishing her senior year of high school.

Rural families needed help on their farms; but after WWII more formal education was soon stressed. My parents, as well as their kin, really encouraged their kids to pursue higher education. I sometimes wonder if some of the hoops that students must jump through to get a certificate before they can work are all that necessary.

12

Yeah for Miss Rensinbrink

Grade school called for some big adjustments for me. I went from being the big boy in charge of activities for my sister "Pooky" and the Bierlink girls to finding my way in the real world of boys and school. My May visit one day to Sumas (soo'-mass) Christian School in 1948 was my whole kindergarten experience. Two things I remember from that day: big, strapping eighth grader Kenny Bosman watched over me on the playground; he seemed protective and heroic. I never dreamed I'd play fastpitch for the Bank of Sumas nine years later with him; now in his mid-80s he's still playing slow-pitch. At the end of my kindergarten day when I came home without my little red baseball cap, my mom didn't appreciate it. I learned to hang on to my hat.

At first my folks would drive me to the end of our road so I could catch a ride on the nauseating diesel-smelling bus; later I usually walked that nearly half a mile. Sometimes I found beer bottles to smash with rocks in the ditch on my way home; later I learned the economic value of collecting beer and pop bottles and turning them in to a local grocery store for a few cents. My first two years of school I spent in an upstairs room on the east end used for first and second graders. Sometimes my ears popped. Alice Likkel, my stern first grade teacher and the principal's wife, liked to use a ruler to slap the palm of the hand of rule violators. The good I experienced the first year of school I would mainly credit to Clarence Schaart, a generous second grader from Abbotsford, B.C.; he often shared a snack with me. Early on, my favorite class was recess. Mostly we played tag, rode the merry-go-round and swings, and played Dare Base and Red Rover in the first couple school years. One "unfavorite" memory occurred in the third grade. Mr. Likkel spanked me right after a recess because I had asked a skinny little first grader named Jackie VanDiest, to retrieve a little board lying on some newly planted grass; printed on a sign were the words, "Stay off the grass!" Jackie helped us out, but I paid the price. Ironically the board Jackie got for our game of Dare Base that recess was very similar to the principal's spanking tool. At home my disrespect to Mom and my sister shown at the dinner table a couple of times led to "warm" visits in the woodshed. Also my one attempt to be an arsonist by lighting a ditch across the road on fire led to another hot date with my dad. I wonder sometimes today about the always "spare the rod" philosophy. Little Johnny was becoming John and learning some important realities; as some say, he learned "where the bear poops in the woods." Some of my harsh punishments served as deterrents that led me to make better choices thereafter. Some of the corporal punishment back then now seems extreme.

My classroom for grades three and four was on the west end of the upstairs of the school. There my favorite-by-far teacher was a lanky, hearty gal with dark eyebrows - Miss Hattie Rensinbrink; she brought warmth and laughter into my grade school experience. She had our class memorize Ps. 103 which we recited in a school program. As she did later with some high school teachers, Mom had Miss Rensinbrink over for dinner and a good time. Mom liked to take pictures; so once during a flood in Sumas she captured Miss Rensinbrink with a teacher friend splashing along in knee-deep water down Main Street and wearing waders and a big smile. Soon at school I noticed my report cards started a pattern that would haunt my school experience for years to come; my grades in science, my least favorite subject, were always my lowest. At recess in the fourth grade I started playing softball when I got my first glove, a Sears' catalogue special. I loved playing 500, a common recess softball game. School was getting better. The rest of my grade school classrooms were on the main floor.

Mrs. Dena VanderStoep, a little old hen and our fifth-grade teacher, brooded over us. I enjoyed the stories about a kid named Ralph she read after the noon break. For grades six through eight my main teacher was the quirky Mr. Joseph Levac from Chicago. Mr. Levac, a flaming red head with pocked cheeks and chin, loved music and physical challenges. When a student in his classroom had a birthday, he'd hold that person over his knee and let all the students give a slap on the "celebrant's" backside, that is, till Sharon Smith hurt her back and the spankings were unceremoniously stopped. Mr. Levac timed all the boys in the sixth through the eighth grade in the 100-yard dash; he took my time on a day when I was wearing engineer boots beneath my chunky legs. My time of 20 seconds flat was the slowest of all the boys; a little better was my 11.3 seconds time at a community track event in my late 30's. Mr. Levac also organized chicken fight tournaments with one person on the back of another to see who could pull the opponents to the ground. Somehow I survived the usual and the unusual during those times.

Often at recess I would play in little competitions in basketball (games of h-o-r-s-e with Anton Mellema) or softball (Yankee/ Dodger pitching duels with Dick Mellema) while most of the boys would goof off or hike out to the bus garage where one thrill led by prankster Billy Verwolf was climbing up onto the rafters so he and his cohorts could pee on an unsuspecting student entering the bus garage for the first time. In our later grade school days some odd nicknames surfaced. Some came from initials like "Medical Donkey" for Merv Dykstra or "Jack Rabbit" for me, but these didn't stick. Other nicknames lasted longer: "Hairless Honk," "Beef," "Itchy Ulcers," and "Phys Ed." Sadly one lad who once came to school with some cow manure on his shoes and was a slower learner was even called a disgusting rhyming nickname. His initials were KJ; I wish I could apologize for mistreating him as I most likely did by calling him that negative name back then. Since then, I've tried to give or use nicknames or pet names that are favorable. Among those grade school classmates was Myron Alsum, now my preferred barber for some forty years.

As a diversion one warm spring afternoon Denny Timmer, an eighth grader, organized a special outing for 12 boys to skip school. We took our bikes for some wonderfully freeing rides in the foothills that splendid afternoon outside of school. But the next day Mr. Levac paddled the rear ends of all of the skippers in front of the seventh and eighth graders' class. I was #11 in the spanking order; waiting through the first ten brought more than one knot to my stomach. My best buddy in grade school, Denny Scheffer, was so scared of what his dad would do if he skipped with us, he was the only boy to stay in school that afternoon with all the girls. Ironically "Schef" probably skipped more days than all the other boys put together when he was in high school as he was not particularly academically motivated then.

The humdrum of school life was broken up for me in more than one way. Playing just a few games each season on the school basketball and fastpitch teams added some spice to school. One privilege I received from Mr. Levac was to be excused from class in the eighth grade to help new classmate Georgie Postma learn to read better; Georgie was a transfer into our eighth-grade class and was quite a storyteller; I don't believe we got much reading done. And as I recall, the young ladies started drawing my attention toward the end of grade school though I was a shy guy. One gal I had my eye on got gulped up by an older high schooler the next year. Our eighth-grade class trip, a visit to Olympia - our state capitol, showed another sacrifice of my dad; he went as a chaperon mainly to help me get up in that one night to help me with my occasional nighttime bladder problem. I guess grade school wasn't all that bad and served me with a pretty solid educational foundation, but I surely anticipated moving on to high school and to see what the new landscape might bring. I'm a tad envious of my younger kin who were wonderfully enfolded in their early educational experiences.

13

Learning to Work

For the oldest boy, work on the farm soon turned from the imaginary to the real. In earlier summers I had spent endless hours picking strawberries, raspberries, pickles, and beans to make a little money. My first check after weeks of tedious, back-breaking strawberry picking for my first summer came to $34.40. My parents let me know some good causes for my $3.44 tithe. Twice a day I helped Dad by feeding the calves and with milking by washing udders and moving the De Laval milking machines from cow to cow in our flat barn. Cleaning out the gutters with a shovel or fork and a wheelbarrow became my regular daily chore. Filling silo with Joe Scheffer on the chopper and my dad at the blower was seasonal custom work; my job was to drive wagons back and forth and help unload them. One summer my parents planted a bean patch to make some Christian school tuition money; that summer our family ate Cheerios for every meal it seemed. The bean poles were good for pole-vaulting, usually; once I tried to vault over a tractor, but the pole cracked in mid-flight, and I hit the deck hard and it nearly shook my innards loose. It also seemed like weeds loved to grow in my dad's huge vegetable garden. Guess who got to pull most of them? On the farm there was not much slack time and lots of learning about life. God was using my folks to train me with their values to honor Him and be responsible by completing the duties I was assigned.

Years later Jeannie and I tried to create small duties for the kids in our suburban or small- town America homes. Those chores in the house or yard were really limited, but we were thankful for the kids' newspaper routes that gave them good training in work accountability in good weather as well as bad. And they certainly appreciated the shekels.

14

Storms A-brewing

Sometimes blowing rather fiercely out of the Fraser Canyon and sweeping through Sumas country, Northeasterns attacked us. For one January 8 my mom had prepared an eighth birthday party for my friends from school and me. It never happened. Newspaper accounts list winds of 75 miles per hour, snow drifts up to 30 feet, and a record low of two degrees. In those days we never spoke of wind chill, but it was really cold. Schools were closed from January 2-28. Instead, my Uncle Elmer's brand new 1950 white Hudson was dragged by chain behind my dad's tractor to the front of our driveway because of fast and high snow accumulation. There it sat for two weeks while Uncle Elmer, Aunt Emma, and cousin Rita had an extended visit playing lots of games, especially caroms, with us inside.

In that snowstorm, as well as in a couple of others, huge snowbanks, sometimes nearly to the height of the house's roof, separated our house from the barn. One time we cut a 25-foot long tunnel out of the snowbank to get straight to the barn instead of making a long circuitous trip over the lower snowbanks out in the pasture. Rides on a sled behind the tractor Dad drove gave us special thrills and spills. When Dad was a boy in the 1920s in Minnesota, his dad had hooked up a car hood to a team of horses to provide exciting rides in the snow.

What happened in America in the late 1960's was another kind of storm. Black Jackie Robinson of the Dodgers had agreed to play for the Brooklyn Dodgers for a whole year and not get in a fight. He accomplished that goal in the 1947 season when he broke the color barrier. But the civil rights movement of the '60's brought lots of protesting and upheaval to our country. The assassination of President Jack Kennedy in 1963 and the deaths of his brother Bobby and Dr. Martin Luther King in 1968 produced lots of unrest in our country. I do remember my Criminology professor cancelling class so we could follow the television news of JFK's death. From my sheltered background I had some wake-up calls as I gradually learned about my own racism. During my college days playing some basketball with massive Buster Mathis, a boxer from Grand Rapids and for a while the heavyweight champ, was my first experience at integration. But that was easy; he was a gentle giant and fun to play against on the basketball court located just off Franklin Street.

Much later, I remember waking up to the news of 9-11-01 as the twin towers in New York were bombed; it was a Tuesday morning before our Men's Prayer and Share time at 6:30 a.m., and half of the men there at the Dutch Mothers' Café had not heard the news before arriving. I had come to this group's meeting since 1983 without such disturbing major news. After the onslaught, America was sent to its knees and some short-term unity resulted. Today concerns fill the hearts and minds of many Americans after all the terrorists' activities and classroom shootings and wild protests, and ugly political bickering and campaigning continue to plague our land. I keep wondering where can we find a servant-leader we can call a true statesman and the polarization within our country can be reduced.

15

Big Stuff

Graduation from Sumas Christian Grade School in 1956 led me to a new school – Lynden Christian High School - and lots of new ventures. The most critical event of my freshman year for me occurred in the late fall. It was "not" big stuff! Selected to the LCHS junior varsity basketball team, Billy Verwolf and I were dropped by the junior varsity coach from what he deemed was a "too large" a team two weeks into the season. I still recall what Cliff Bajema said to me at a restroom visit; "It should've been me" as well as a comforting word from Jim VanderMay. This shock rocked my boat but soon helped me to clarify some of my priorities in life: sports weren't everything after all! Fortunately the next season I rebounded to become a junior varsity starter while Billy played on a varsity basketball team in Chicago, where his dad had moved to a new pastorate. In Dutch enclaves, gyms were maybe built as much for basketball, maybe even more than for physical education, so that lanky kids often from Dutch forebears could flourish ever after Calvin College had given its approval for the sport around 1920. Basketball possibly first seemed "holier" than other sports to many constituents.

My last three years of high school I really started to feel a part of the action. My sophomore year at LC yielded some fruit for "Rosae Fruitex" (Rose Tree) as I was called by Rev. J.K. Van Baalen in a Latin II class of all upperclassmen but me. So I was called "Fruiti" for a while. Playing basketball under Coach John Fakkema and baseball under Coach Garris Timmer for LC helped me feel included and valued. Gradually I sensed how participation and performance in sports helped my growing self-acceptance and confidence and led to a lot of joy. And getting my driver's license was a grand freedom to me, but my first traffic ticket was humbling. My sophomore year a friendship with Bob Oordt began to develop; he was one welcoming Lynden kid. At the end of the year, after an encouraging push from junior Gordy Buys, a former Ebenezer school sports' opponent, I ran for and was chosen as the student council's vice-president. I also took my first official date, a Sumas gal, to the Pep Club banquet. That year was topped off by attending, as the area's rep, the then Young Calvinist (now Youth Unlimited) Convention held in Edmonton, Alberta. There I met Dr. Peter Eldersveld, the rich Back-to-God-Hour voice, not unlike the "golden throat" of Vin Scully for Dodger broadcasts. Our family listened to Dr. Eldersveld over the radio every Sunday when I was growing up, but when I saw him up close, I could barely believe such a beautiful big voice could come out of such a short man who smoked stogies. My sophomore year at LCHS had broadened me in several ways, and the temptations then seemed limited.

Receiving our family's second car, a 1951 two-toned green Chevy, as my own wheels gave me more independence and freedom for the last two years of high school. I spent most of my 1958 Christmas vacation on a basketball team trip to California. We beat Ripon Christian in Ripon (and I had my only good blind date after the game there) and won two games at Valley Christian in Bellflower, where we upset the Crusaders for the tournament championship in a low scoring affair, 46-34. It is very possible that my future wife Jeannie, then a freshman there, was sitting in the stands and even rooting against the Lyncs! A very good opposing player was the Crusaders' sophomore Art Hommes, whose heirs would make a big impression in LCHS sports and beyond much later. Manager Jim "Snimps" Wynstra taught me how to play chess in the back seat of a car on that trip; many years later our children became pretty proficient at playing chess and won significant money in the local Theresa Tromp Chess Tournaments. Having freshman sister "Pooky" in high school was a sure aide for my social life as I began dating more broadly. After my junior year I was chosen to attend Boys' State in Tacoma at Pacific Lutheran University, where student leaders gathered for a two-day experience. I was busy learning about the importance of participation and leadership.

At age 17 I started my senior year, a time of important decisions. On September 27, 1959 I made my public profession of faith in Jesus Christ before my Sumas church family; since my dad was serving as an elder, my family and I treasured that experience. At school I served as the senior class president. Donna Veltkamp became my special girlfriend for much of my senior year. In my English class each week Merle Meeter, a unique teacher who loved his bar bells and heavy lifting, provided challenging vocabulary tests that spurred on my appreciation for words and their power. My interest in journalism led me to become the sports editor of the Hilite. In a course called "Ref Doc" students discussed the rightness or wrongness of space travel and movie attendance, conflicting issues of the time. Playing cards, dancing, and going to movies were viewed as worldly pursuits by my church's denomination in those pre-TV days. That was then; this is now, a time when discretion is needed. My swan song with my Cornet was playing "Trumpet Voluntary" at the graduation for our class of 70. Brother Ger picked up my horn and blessed many by playing it and by using his voice and directing ability as well.

What I had learned about Jesus and the Bible at home was quite nicely complemented by my Christian education. Learning the distinction between Christianity and all the other religions of the world was useful; only in Christianity is God rescuing the lost and the lost can't earn heaven by doing something good or by not doing anything too bad. By faith I accepted Jesus as my Savior; that gave me eternal life insurance. But learning to know Jesus as my friend and Lord took a lot longer. And for the eternal gift I have received I still ask, "Why me, Lord?"

In school and elsewhere I have learned how those who are in the power positions or traditionally important groups often have little idea of what those outside the circles of advantage or power experience. Students with lots of kin nearby often have a big edge. Without any supervision outside, there were lots of inequities on the playgrounds.

Nearly ready to graduate I received a big surprise. For my first semester at LCHS I had had a rare freshman schedule. Beyond the regular courses that freshmen took, I found on my plate Latin I and Band instead of a study hall and General Science. That choice caught up with me just before I was to graduate. The superintendent, the visionary and venerable Mark Vander Ark – sometimes called "Blue Beard," called me into his office to declare I had missed three required courses – General Science, Geometry, and Church History. After some pondering to resolve the problem, he suggested I write a 500-word paper on John Calvin. I appreciated that remedy, and I graduated without the three required courses, likely the only LCHS student with such an omission. Things probably have tightened up a bit in the registrar's office after my situation. After lots of huffing and puffing besides some staggering literally and figuratively, I finally, with God's help, reached the first base of my life with my high school graduation. Thinking I was on top of the world, I soon discovered I was a long way from getting to second base.

16

Heroes

My first childhood hero was definitely my dad; I sometimes literally tried to walk in his boots and footsteps. I really looked up to him. In late grade school I looked up to some high schoolers. With my sports' infatuation I soon started to admire big time athletes - in baseball Duke Snider of the Dodgers, in basketball Elgin Baylor of the Lakers, and in football Paul Hornung of the Packers. I surely put Jackie Robinson on a pedestal for what he endured in 1947 when he broke the color barrier in baseball as a Dodger. Every April 15, the date when Jackie agreed to sign a unique contract, every major league baseball player today honors his memory and courage and break-through by wearing #42 in games. Former M's Ken Griffey, Jr. is credited with starting this tradition.

Already as a youngster I had biblical heroes - David from the Old Testament and Paul from the New Testament, certainly men with feet of clay, men who needed repentance but who were used mightily by God in His kingdom. So our sons carry the names of David and Paul. I have long admired Joshua and Daniel too. Dr. Peter Eldersveld of the Back-to-God Hour every Sunday morning had an impressive voice and message that I admired, and in college Chaplain Ben Pekelder made chapels come alive with his fictional character of F.o.g (feet on ground) and his learning through relevant college experiences. I have always admired Billy

Graham with his campaigns and outreach. So many inspirational writers such as James Dobson and Max Lucado and Philip Yancey also have richly impacted me. I am thankful for all the positive influences that substantially affected me.

17

Challenges

At 50 years of age, I received a challenge from my visiting Aunt Harriet, some years older. To the Hemlock Ski Resort across the Canadian border we went. I put on the cumbersome gear and after some practice moved up to the bunny hill. There I made two booboos. Once when I was riding the chairlift, one of my skis dropped off; so naturally I jumped off my seat into the snow, about four feet below, to retrieve it. Some authority with a loudspeaker really bawled me out. Later in the day when I thought I was improving as a skier, I gathered too much speed coming down the hill and forgot how to snowplow. All I could do was use an old baseball technique, a bent leg slide, to stop. The problem is that I showered a lot of people along the way with snow before I came to rest. That was my first and last day of snow-skiing. I wasn't much better in my few attempts at waterskiing earlier either. I guess skiing is not one of my gifts.

A few years later I was 57. In 1999 Lynden held its first Raspberry Festival with the blazing heat bouncing off Front Street; it featured lots of three-on-three basketball tournament games and raspberry sundaes. It was a thrill for me when our team of Rick Holleman, Rocky Mouw, my son Dave, and me won the adult recreation division's championship on a long "bomb" from Rocky in overtime. Playing with "jumping jack" son Dave was really special. Playing in that tournament was a challenge I was glad I had accepted.

Now at age 77 and still recovering from a hip surgery, I'm hopeful and eager sometime to give my five-year old grandson "Dookie" the experience of coming in second place in a foot race. First I have to heal well.

18

Play Ball

Playing with tractors and trucks as a tyke drew my attention for a while until I started playing ball. After I got my first glove, I'd repeatedly fire a rubber ball against the west side of the barn and field it. A normal person would view my doing this over and over as monotony, but I loved it. Dad liked to go the auction barn sales on Tuesday when I was a kid, and he'd invite me to go along. But usually the ball won over the auction. Quite often after the cows were milked and the chores were all done, Dad would hit me softball flies and grounders if he didn't have to go to one meeting or another.

I spent hours by the end of the driveway hitting marble-sized stones there that were perfect to whack with my bat, an old broom handle. Our small pasture to the north of the barn provided a perfect size for my imaginary diamond. In left field there was a fence. In right field stood the barn; it was a home run over the barn and a double off it. I concocted line-ups for games in which my favorite team would win. One day I smacked a line drive through a window of the milk house in front of the barn. That mistake did not occur again. Hitting stones and imitating pro baseball players is how I learned to switch hit. Living on a farm without neighbors nearby required a kind of inventiveness to create games. Since I grew up without little league sports, I couldn't be jealous of kids getting to play organized games. But I surely enjoyed the freshness and competition of real games later.

Dad first mounted a hoop for me to play basketball by the milk house. My favorite place for a hoop was in the hay mow of the barn when enough of the alfalfa was removed. I spent lots of hours shooting hoops. In the fourth grade I started to spend recess periods playing 500 with my classmates. Like me, the Timmer and Mellema brothers and others enjoyed playing ball too. Getting invited by friend Denny Timmer to watch in his Clearbrook home near Nooksack High School my first major league baseball game on television was quite a thrill. Game seven of the 1954 World Series went to the New York Giants, who upset the favored Cleveland Indians, and in game one Willie Mays made his amazing catch in deep centerfield at the Polo Grounds. Seeing that game helped me visualize even better from the radio coverage the following year when the Dodgers beat the Yankees in the series for the first time as I cleaned out calf pens. I still recall the Gillette razor blades' commercial of "Feel sharp, look sharp, and be sharp." Playing ball has enriched my adult life in many ways. Baseball fans always anticipate the fresh start of a new game when they hear the words, "Play ball!"

Playing recreational basketball, fastpitch, and baseball as an adult has connected me to a huge variety of acquaintances and friends. Playing with Rick Holleman in an over-35 basketball tournament in 1986 led to the first of two championship trophies in Nanaimo on Vancouver Island. In '87 I received the MVP award after going 9-16 with 4 extra base hits as our church fastpitch team won the tournament. Alumni games were fun. I found one old newspaper clipping with this headline: "Rozeboom's HR lifts LC alums to win." Hitting so few long balls, it's rather funny I don't remember that three-run jack, but the newspaper says it did happen in an LC alumni baseball game in the '80's.

Playing ball can be so freeing while being so intense. It's the feeling of being a kid again. It's a great escape from the important responsibilities of life even if it may bring some agony or ecstasy. For me it has brought a whole bevy of connections and many moments of special joy.

19

Learning to Lead

Other than my leadership with my younger sister and her neighbor friends I don't think I was a natural leader. Being the oldest sibling led to some leading of others, I guess. I did not really relish being in leadership positions, but when pressed into responsible positions I did learn something about leadership. I was chosen as the young peoples' society president in my Sumas church. This led to a privilege, being sent to the Young Calvinists' convention in Edmonton one summer. Recruited and nudged by Gordy Buys into the vice-presidency of student council, I watched my friend Jim VanderMay operate as president. Going to Boys' State at PLU in Tacoma got me in touch with lots of high school leaders throughout the state just prior to my senior year. Running a few class meetings as the senior class president with the advice of Mr. Ben Boxum, the humble Kansas storyteller and teacher, taught me how to lead a large group. On athletic teams I showed younger players how to practice and play hard. One day Larry Hagan, our choir director, had me direct the choir for one song. There were lots of promptings.

In college I had a side job with Grey Y helping Al Stremler as we directed elementary age kids during the afterschool hours. Organizing my own intramural teams in college was fun and natural for me. High school teaching forced me to be a classroom leader, and at both high schools in which I taught I was asked to serve as the head of the English department. Serving as an elder on church councils several times led to a chairmanship. Often Jeannie and I have teamed to be small group leaders in our church fellowship.

As a coach I had to lead my teams. My goal was to be organized but flexible in getting the job done. In the 2017 summer I organized a reunion of my high school baseball teammates of 57 years earlier; the stories were good even if possibly not all totally true. After retirement I got a monthly meeting going for former LCHS teachers. And I still provide a little leadership to our Tuesday morning men's Prayer and Share group. When I look back, I see I've been in a leadership position some of the time, not that I crave it.

20

College Experience

In the fall of 1960, I joined some of my fellow LCHS graduates to attend Calvin College, now renamed as Calvin University. Much later I learned from my folks that they had prayed me there. Driving by car, sometimes straight through, to Grand Rapids, Michigan each time brought some of its own memories. My freshman year I roomed with Bob Oordt, a high school friend and teammate. Our home that first year consisted only of a bedroom with a community bathroom across the hall in a home owned by a person who predicted that if John F. Kennedy were to be elected, we'd all be Communists soon. Well, I learned lots of perspectives, and college became a very broadening experience. Getting used to the long Michigan winters required adjusting, but meeting lots of great kids, several of whom became friends, was wonderful for this country kid; playing freshman basketball and varsity baseball stretched me too. It's fair to say I did not major in academics my first year of college. As a sophomore I lived with former high school friend Jim Vander May and several others on the second floor of a house on Henry Street near Bates church. In high school we called him "Fenimore," but Jim was called "Polyphemus" by our Latin teacher because he tried to do a head stand before one basketball practice; after his arms collapsed, he ended up wearing a big patch over his healing head cuts. After a career of working at Pine Rest,

Jim has written a couple of worthy junior-high level books about bullying.

When Christmas was nearing in my sophomore year, I planned to stay in Grand Rapids. Funds did not seem to be there so I could go home for Christmas. But Bob Oordt arrived in GR just as vacation was beginning. He had dropped out of Calvin after his freshman year and began rolling in the dough by working at Boeing in Seattle. He earned enough to buy a brand new '62 Volkswagen with its outstanding gas mileage so he could visit his kin in Kentucky and Michigan. Before he headed back to Washington, he offered me a deal – ride and drive back to WA with him, split the gas costs, and worry about getting back later. Since I longed to go home, I hopped in the car with him and began the two-day trek west over lots of snow and ice. Candy bars and pop at gas stations was our food. Outside of Willmar, Minnesota we ran out of gas just two miles from town. The penetrating wind chill was some 20 degrees below zero and the time was 3:30 a.m. We tried pushing the car a little way but were so relieved when a drunk going home from a party saw our need, helped us get gas, and put us on our way. Pretty much the pattern was that I would drive four hours and then sleep four hours for the whole trip. After 46 hours I surprised my family at home. My share of the cost for the trip was a happy $13.50. However, I had to lie on the floor with an unhappy belly ache from all the tension for almost two days before I could enjoy Christmas with my family.

My parents let me take to college the 1951 two-toned green Chevy Power Glide for my junior year. I had it painted black and named it "Midnight." Having wheels at Calvin certainly increased my freedom and independence. "Midnight" had such a strong battery that I often gladly jumpstarted the engines of my several neighbors on our street when a really cold streak hit Grand Rapids that winter. Sadly death came to "Midnight" when it blew a rod in the middle of nowhere, actually 25 miles from Columbus, Montana my senior year as sister "Pooky" and three guys accompanied me to Calvin. We were forced to find a hotel for one night before I could purchase a '49 Olds with a big steering wheel and Wyoming license plates. My junior year I lived with Ken Terpstra from Seattle and Dave Schelhaas and Virg Vis from Edgerton till Paul Beezhold from Seattle replaced Virg. Playing Pinochle almost every noon for a good hour gave us a nice break from studying. For my senior year 1110 Thomas became my home along with the "inmates" - Ken Terpstra, Gord Hassing, Denny Brasser, Jim Harkema, Dave Wagner, Tom Smedes and Art Frens. Some of our water fights were legendary. I loved having a shower in the basement since I never had that privilege before. Wagner-inspired as I recall, our papermache display won first prize for that year's homecoming. Living with a variety of interesting personalities required some coping skills, but "Brass" and "Wags" became lifelong friends.

During my years at Calvin I was impressed by several professors – Howard Rienstra in history, John H Bratt in a Bible course, Stanley Wiersma and Steve Vander Weele in English, and Don Wilson in anthropology. Wilson really stretched my perspective of the creation story. In contrast one blinking education professor was the dullest possible instructor I've ever had. But I did learn a lot. I wasn't so much piling up knowledge and wisdom as learning that a little education shows how much more is beyond it. At the end of my sophomore year Dr. Barney Steen, my advisor, suggested I major in English so I could help change the common stereotype of the old maid English teacher and around my English teaching do some coaching.

My social life became much richer and fuller and sweeter after meeting a certain gal just before Christmas of my senior year. With football and basketball intramurals providing a blast, my final year just sailed along.

During my college summers I did various kinds of work. During high school summers I had often milked for vacationing farmers. And I continued doing some more of that. One summer my Grampa DeKoekkoek hired me to work on his Everson area farm; I really enjoyed my work there highlighted by drinking his homemade root beer and downing Gram's fresh cookies. Another summer I worked for Gay Digerness, a gentleman farmer, on his Sumas farm – milking, haying, and filling silo. The next summer with a couple of Sumas off-duty policemen I helped tear down and rebuild a good chunk of the Everson Auction barn; that job paid a then envious $2.00 per hour. Playing lots of fastpitch softball during those summer nights gave some levity to the "heavity." I played ball for the Bank of Sumas and Lynden Auction teams 1957 through 1964 after sitting on the bench for DeBoer Hatchery as a ninth grader with Denny and Ronnie Timmer. Fastpitch, for a long time a major recreational draw, was still pretty much in its heyday in the area, but sadly its popularity seemed to decline with the advent of slow-pitch and other options around the century's turn.

Academic work and manual jobs along with good times of play gave me lots of growing experiences. I shall always be thankful for my parents' prayers that propelled me to Calvin College. I was busy absorbing a wonderful world-and-life view. I was proud to graduate as a Calvin Knight and heed my callling.

Getting to second base in my trip around the bases took lots of wise advisors, blessings, and perseverance. I had no idea how long it would take for me to get to third base.

21

"Snooky"

<hr>

Before my senior year I asked sister Ida Ann ("Pooky"), my good friend since high school, to give me a list of five or six girls that she thought might make good prospects for me to consider as a potential bride; her thoughtful pre-marital help became extremely beneficial. "Pooky" must have forgiven me for years of my teasing her, sometimes relentlessly. On a triple date at a December basketball game I came with one gal of the list, but I met another, also from the list – Jeannie (born Virginia Mae De Jong), a delightfully delicate, cheerful, and talented sophomore girl from Bellflower, California. A few days later and after an unofficial coffee date when she wore a saucy tam, I took her on a Friday, the 13th, to a symphony for our first official date, and I never looked back; all my general dating was done. I do recall taking her to meet my seven roommates at 1110 Thomas for the first time was quite a challenging venture.

After Calvin baseball games we often ate hamburgers at a fast food spot called Zingers on 28th Street across from Bill Knapp's. And we often visited Jeannie's Uncle Clarence and Aunt Mary, jovial folks who had moved from Iowa. That summer Jeannie met my family in Washington; then I drove her down to California and visited her family there. One morning at 7:30 I dropped her off at Knotts' Berry Farm, where she worked in the Cable Car Kitchen. I drove the 21 hours from Buena Park to Seattle before deciding I needed a nap so I could arrive home on the farm for breakfast. I woke up from my "nap" on a Seattle service station parking lot at 2:30 in the afternoon with the sun streaming into the car and a fly buzzing around inside the car. To say I wasn't too happy was right. I did join my folks that evening for supper.

Jeannie has been the delight and joy of my life as well as my anchor in so many respects. Many years later, my last South Christian High School students said Mrs. Rozeboom had been the best teacher they ever had. They loved her as their first-grade teacher which is the level where she served for her first two years after college.

The next October with a little bubbly we were engaged on a Friday, the 13th by Reeds' Lake; she loved her marquise ring. The proposal occurred in "Jeremiah," the blue '49 Olds with Wyoming license plates I had bought in Montana; it had replaced "Midnight" when its engine died before my senior year. The next August on a Friday, the 13th I was thrilled to marry the love of my life, the third daughter of Gerrit and Gerdena DeJong and sibling to Art, Kathleen (Andrews) and Phyllis (Witsken) in Bellflower at Jeannie's home church. It was a toasty evening when Rev. Walter Ackerman hitched us. When we exchanged the wedding rings, we each said the same vow: "I give this ring as a symbol of my constant faithfulness and abiding love." Jeannie's friend, Larry Bouma, drove the get-away car. "Sugar Lump," our white '61 Ford Fairlane and our only ever non-GM product, had replaced "Jeremiah" for our transportation the first couple years of our marriage; it carried us from a Long Beach hotel the first night and then on to Santa Barbara, "the American Riviera," for our honeymoon week. Nearly drowning in a hotel pool on your honeymoon is not a good idea; both the new bride and groom were grateful a big strapping fellow under a nearby canopy hauled me out of the deep end. We ended our honeymoon at a Dodger baseball game. From its inception, our romance has been and continues to be very gratifying, even when we have experienced a few deep waters.

And the gift that Jeannie has been for me has just kept on giving. She brought three bright-eyed infants into the world and served as their loving mother without too much smother. She worked as a stay-at-home mom and as an employee outside of our home once the kids were all in school. She has been a friend to many and has no harsh words for anyone. She has blessed every community she's been a part of with her cheerfulness and sweetness. She's been my companion and confidante. I prize her as a gift like no one else on earth.

Here's an entry from a writing course I participated in during the 2009 winter. The description is entitled, "The First Time I Kissed Her." This is the rest of the "story" – The first time I kissed Jeannie was memorable. The coop door in the cramped entry way smiled. Angels rejoiced. Earlier that evening's symphony special music was wonderfully relaxing. But now my heart went pitter patter and faster. My blood pressure rose as I touched those cherry lips. Her head tilted and my soul yearned for her. Friday, the 13th would never be the same.

Tradition was built upon the Friday, 12.13.63 foundation, our first date. The next Valentines' Day knocked me over. Love abounded and my inspired 229 bowling score was my zenith score in bowling by far. Today Jeannie still tastes great and is no less filling. Love still pours out of her eyes and lips. She's my inspiration and sweetheart, my "Snooky!" and she amazes me in so many ways.

22

Teams and Coaches

To play on a real team to this solo shooter/hitter after lots of imaginary games was very enjoyable. In the seventh and eighth grade I played a few games of basketball and softball for Sumas Christian School. Our hoops' coach, Ted Vander Mey, I especially appreciated. I can still smell his Mennon's aftershave and his cigarette breath as he coached us on the outside cement court. Very competitive, Ted taught us some tricks of the trade. He tried to prepare us to play Ebenezer, another small country school, with its two stars – big Al "Buck" Stremler, about a half taller than I was at that age, and quick Gordy Buys. We wanted to prove that we the Wildcats in our new stiff maroon and gold uniforms could outplay the "Lemon Squeezers" in their shorts or swimming trunks. I drew the assignment of guarding big "Buck" using Ted's techniques. But the boys of Ebenezer proved to be the clearly better team as they surely outmuscled and out-quicked us in that one big game.

As a freshman at Lynden Christian High School I made the junior varsity basketball team. However, making it and staying on it were too different things. After two weeks the then coach, Lee Vander Ark, decided his team had too many players; he dropped Billy Verwolf and me, the two boys from the Sumas area, after two weeks into the season. But he added another boy named Richie, who "needed it" because he had just come out of a detention program. This double move really surprised me, but it helped me to clarify some of values and priorities. The next season found Billy playing on a varsity team in Chicago, where his family had moved, and me playing on the J.V. first five for Coach John Fakkema, a coach I really enjoyed. The first five, or six, always got to ride with him in his car to away games, all in Canada. On these long rides he shared pieces of his philosophies of life and offered wise advice for us teenage boys – Bob Oordt, Sherm Polinder, Ken Haak, Harry Stuurmans, Cecil Stuurmans, and me. On the court he helped us master his "rubber band" zone defense. Joining the mop up unit in one varsity game, I got the ball about 15' down the baseline to the right of the hoop for a wide open jump shot; my first varsity shot suffered from too slow a release as the ball was swatted out of bounds into the curtain on the stage. I had lots to learn.

For all my varsity action in high school in basketball and baseball Garris Timmer was my coach. Called "Chrome Dome" by some, he had been a very good athlete in high school and college. By the time I was a senior a major change in athletic competition occurred at LCHS. For the first time, at mid-year, our school was accredited so that LC sports teams were permitted to play against the public schools of our state; before this change we had basically only played Canadian schools. During the winter our basketball team played a couple of nonleague games with Nooksack and Mt. Baker. The bands of our county team opponents played "When the saints go marching in" at each of their home games with the Lyncs. With my ability to shoot hook shots with either hand Coach Timmer put me at the center position. I was often called upon to set screens for Harold Terpstra, our veteran guard. In only one game did I play against a center with my 6'1" height; in that game I managed to score 28 points. In one radio broadcast interview one of my teammates told Haynes Fey I was the hardest worker on the team. I recall Coach Timmer had to kick talented sophomore Ken Faber and me out of the gym more than once after practice was over; we loved to play and practice. I have always believed a ballplayer should earn his position on a team through showing his skill and effort, not because he was entitled to it. Thus I always appreciated coaches who let the best player play.

My sophomore and junior seasons of LC baseball were skimpy with only a few games scheduled. Since most of us had grown up playing fastpitch softball, we slowly picked up the nuances of baseball play. Lots of drama filled our senior year. Our baseball team was now a member of the Whatcom County League with its seven teams. Our entire infield was composed of seniors - Polinder at 1B, Kok ("Beep") at 2B, Terpstra at SS, and Rozeboom at 3B.

When Coach Timmer said we would not have practice on a Friday, some of us seniors rallied the troops to have batting practice at least. I enjoyed hitting second in the batting order. In the historic first meeting between Lynden Public and Lynden Christian on April 12, 1960, we the visiting Lyncs (Lyn C S) rallied to defeat the Lions in extra innings. The <u>Lynden Tribune</u> stated over 500 fans witnessed the game on Lynden's field behind the Darigold plant. My eventual brother-in-law John Vander Molen, our sophomore southpaw, pitched the complete game win that day. Finishing the season in a tie for first place meant we were co-champions in LCHS's first try ever for any WCL sport.

At Calvin College I played junior varsity basketball as a freshman and four seasons of baseball under Coach Don Vroon. To make the basketball team every player had to run a four-mile cross country course in under 30 minutes. I managed to come in third of all the prospects despite carrying 195 pounds after consuming too many desserts in the dining hall. But my lack of height, ball handling skills, and quickness hampered my playing time. Later Coach Vroon let me play inside again, and I made a few crowd-pleasing hook shots. In practice sessions guarding big lefty Ralph Honderd was a big test; he could shoot outside and drive well. I discovered playing intramurals the next three years was so much fun.

When I turned out as a freshman for baseball, Coach Vroon probably misjudged my skill level after I hit a couple doubles in a scrimmage. For my first hit deep into the 6-hole, I stumbled out of the batter's box and was called "4.9" for a while, my home to 1B time. My best time later was 4.2 seconds. Undeservedly, I played every inning of every game that year even though I batted under the Mendoza line. The truth is my freshman season I had a strong arm and good backhand but made too many fielding errors as balls were often rifled to me at shortstop. It wasn't until my junior season when Coach moved me to the pasture that I became a hitter. Learning to hit the college curve ball really took time. Going on spring training trips to Indiana, Tennessee, and Florida was broadening. One spring, meeting some Southern belles was charming, but I wasn't too comfortable on the dance floor in Hoosier country. My best game as a junior was a home game against Kalamazoo College. I stung the Hornets' pitcher with three hits, each of them glancing off his glove or body. As a senior I had my best season. Logic says it was because my girlfriend Jeannie was in the bleachers and maybe because I was wearing my favorite number 13 on my back. After batting .345, I was selected to the all-conference team as an outfielder. My only collegiate home run was a grand slam of 400 feet over the centerfield fence at Knollcrest; student manager Jerry Terpsma, also our baseball scorekeeper at Lynden Christian earlier, was able to retrieve that ball for me. Some of my teammates were interesting characters – Rich "Mouth" Hofman (Florida's winningest HS baseball coach), husky voiced Dan Lagestee, and goofy Phil "Rebel" Van Slooten among others. Our team loved singing in the showers.

Besides playing school ball, I played fastpitch with a variety of coaches and teammates till I turned 60. Playing ball showed me the need to be a supportive teammate. Watching all the coaches I had led me to take and apply from them what seemed good. A key to every team's success is mastering the fundamentals. Though offense gets the glory more times than not, the importance of solid defense cannot be overrated. In high school baseball, for sure, more games are lost than won. Making mental and physical errors and putting runners on base without the virtue of a hit are critical downfalls for losing teams. I have long appreciated the emphasis on small ball that I learned first in recreational fastpitch; the importance of making contact as a batter and knowing how to execute bunts and run-and-hit plays along with good baserunning skills don't seem to be in vogue today at the major league level with its "boom or bust" approach, but they were my allies in coaching.

Tommy Lasorda, the veteran Dodger manager, said managing a team is like holding a bird in your hand; "Hold it too tight and it is squeezed to death; hold it too loosely and it flies away." Somewhere between being a players' coach and a Vince Lombardi authoritarian is what I eventually aimed for as a coach. I tried to apply the principle of being organized but flexible for my high school teaching and coaching.

With AAU and traveling youth teams today have sports' packed schedules, often around which entire families live their weekends, I wonder lots about over-emphasis and burn out concerns. Former major league player and manager Dusty Baker advised young ball players to be well-rounded by playing as many different sports as possible, getting as many different coaches as possible, and learning as many different skills as possible. To specialize early in a single sport he thought was unwise. So much general learning could be missed; and so much broader appreciation for various sports later limited. There could be a burnout factor or overuse syndromes. And he said, "If an athlete is any good by the time he's finished with high school, the cream will rise to the top."

23

Reading, Writing, but no "Rithmetic"

After completing my practice teaching under professor Bill Hendricks in the '64 spring, I was relieved to receive a contract to teach at South Christian High School in Cutlerville, a little south of Grand Rapids, Michigan. My salary was $4,500. At the Town Talk service station gas was only 23 cents a gallon. I had interviewed for a Holland Christian junior high position and was very thankful to be offered two contracts after two interviews during my busy spring of practice teaching, getting to know Jeannie better, and playing baseball for my final season at Calvin College. I believe higher hands were leading me since landing a teaching job in Michigan was often very difficult. I was being called.

Where we lived did not define us, but in those homes lots of lesson plans and correcting of papers and tests occurred. For my first year of teaching I lived in a "pinchy" apartment in Kelloggsville with Dick "Woody" Woudstra, an old acquaintance. The next year as a married couple Jeannie and I lived in a rental house in a sometimes suspect neighborhood on Delaware Street in Grand Rapids. Our routine evening break included watching a 10:00 p.m. television program – "Run for Your Life" on Mondays, "The Fugitive" on Tuesdays, and "I Spy" on Wednesdays. We thought Bill Cosby was great then. We celebrated our first anniversary by using a saved up $10, our weekly allowance for groceries, for a dinner date at Safee's, then a restaurant on Division Avenue. We enjoyed our steaks but had to drink only water so we could cover the bill. The next year we rented a home on Willard Street in Cutlerville before buying our first home on Herbert Street, a very handy stone's throw from SCHS. The $13,900 cost of that place seemed to be a large investment at the time. After a couple years there our family moved to a home without a garage on Fendale just south of Pine Rest Hospital; that place cost us $35,900. There we lived until our move west in August of 1978,

I began what turned into a 42-year career with some definite trepidation. I had heard stories about teachers who were run out of their classrooms by rowdy students. But advice from and friendships with the likes of Don and Alyce Boender, Henry Baron, and Ed Start helped me survive my first couple years at SCHS. As a rookie English teacher, being assigned to teach mostly unmotivated non-college prep students and using outdated textbooks left for me a hefty challenge. Assigned to be the sponsor for homecoming my first year there was another venture since the governor of Michigan had crowned the homecoming queen the year before. Appreciation by students for well turned expressions and insights in literature did not seem all that common. Teaching brought definite challenges early in my career. But I did survive, as did my students.

Every year I taught sophomores a basic writing course, without a textbook, of course, beyond the Warriner's grammar "Bible." For the setting for some of the class's writing assignments I had the class members choose a locale for a setting. One student with the initials of MH suggested this place - "The rolling hills of Vagina." I really couldn't share that option with the class. Many of my 14 years at SCHS I taught American Literature. In the mid-'70's, and only for a couple years, the English department ambitiously carved the English curriculum into 36 nine-week courses. Teaching courses such as Social Protest Literature, Vocabulary Enrichment, Science Fiction, Robert Frost Poetry, and others stretched me. The smorgasbord approach was intended to create more interest for the students; and it did, for a while, but then more traditional courses were recalled for easier scheduling. On Saturdays and during summers of the early 1970's, I finished the classes for my master's degree, a combination of English and Physical Education with Coaching, at Western Michigan University in Kalamazoo. I had added a brown and yellow Bronco to my identities.

One fall I had a bright-eyed, but sweet-natured young man in my English class at SCHS. Brian Diemer, already an outstanding cross country and track athlete, was a junior and wanted to know if I thought he should play basketball; he said he'd probably be a back-up guard on the varsity team. He did follow, for his junior year, my suggestion that he could be more well-rounded if he played basketball instead of just running so far ahead in all his races. However, his specialization after in running events took him through the University of Michigan all the way to the 1984 Olympics, where he competed in and won a bronze medal in the steeplechase besides serving as a captain for the entire American delegation. Since 1986, for some thirty plus years, he has faithfully led Calvin College's cross-country teams to accomplish incredible success in the MIAA and in the postseason on the national scene as well.

In 1967 we purchased "Honey Bear," our spanking new navy blue Olds Cutless with a black vinyl top; it cost us $3600. That durable car carried the two of us to Baltimore, Maryland where I studied for that summer at Morgan State University, predominantly a black college, on an NDEA grant. A few years earlier the country provided NSF grants for science and math teachers so America could compete with Russia in the space age race. NDEA grants for teachers of history and English became available shortly thereafter. After our Baltimore experience, which included a trip to the Smithsonian and other sites in Washington, D.C., we drove the 3000 miles to the west coast to visit kin. After all the winding roads and switchbacks of West Virginia, we got to St. Louis. The 80 miles per hour speed limit on the freeway from Kansas heading toward Denver was a super switch. Leaving the VanderMolens and our new niece Jacki in Denver a little too late one morning meant traveling through California's Mojave Desert in the hot afternoon. With no air conditioning, we sucked on ice cubes over that forlorn stretch of nearly 200 miles. The temperature reached 123 degrees that day there. But we made the best of our coast-to-coast trip and return to Michigan.

To bring home the bacon, I spent a couple summers working for the De Vries family-owned Burton Aluminum. Over and over I heard the tedious song, "Taking Care of Business." But most of my Michigan summers I spent employed by Flier Underground Sprinkling Systems (FUSS). There also I worked under one of my former students who "schooled" me as we installed sprinkling systems. To add some enjoyment to the work, I arranged to have trivia contests with three different workers that I was often paired with. History, Bible, and sports were the categories that my specialized cohorts and I used. One of my last summer workdays in Michigan I was saved from serious injury by Bob Blacquiere, who had been my former high school student and ball player.

Starting with our 25th wedding anniversary, Jeannie and I began a rhythm of special trips with Don and Marcia Steeby, our precious MI friends. We enjoyed celebration trips – for our 25th to Hawaii, our 30th to Las Vegas, our 35th to Spain, our 40th to Italy, and our 45th to Yalapa by Puerto Vallerta. In case there is no baseball in heaven, I know I can deal with it; there was no evidence of baseball in Spain, Italy, or Yelapa, and I did just fine.

We were stretched in these trips by engaging a variety of peoples, places, and cultures. Together with the Steebys we shared many treasured times.

In 1978 after 14 years at SCHS, Lynden Christian High School beckoned. I was especially encouraged to come to LCHS by former Hudsonville Unity teacher, the energetic Harlan Kredit, as well as two Lynden Christian School board members. They challenged me to help make a difference at LC; drugs had invaded the 1970's LC culture. By moving to the west coast, our kids could now live by one set of grandparents. Jeannie bravely led the way by maneuvering "the Red Chariot," our '71 Chevy Kingswood station wagon with our tent trailer attached, and I drove "Pumpkin Patch," a large orange U-haul truck, for the 2400-mile trip. We used walkie talkies for communication.

In Lynden we were warmly received by and cast our lot with the fellowship at Third CRC. Changing from an anticipated $19,000 salary at SCHS to the $16,000 one at LCHS soon became a financial challenge for us; the cost of living besides our full tuition cost was much higher in the Pacific Northwest. Our new home cost us $52,500; it had two bathrooms and a fireplace, Jeannie's wishes. My parents helped us to "make it" with their generous financial support. Having coached and guided my life well in my youth, they became a rich encouragement as well as supportive fans at my games.

In my 28-year hitch at LCHS, I taught some of the same courses as before. A favorite writing assignment was using the five-paragraph with three major influences' paper for my sophomores; they had to do some wholesome reflecting. Another particularly gratifying assignment was the providential point-of-view paper that followed the inspiration of William Bradford's perspective in colonial America and finding God's hand in hard times. My students shared often powerfully out of the wells of their own and their family's experiences in this confidential assignment. My mark for a good work choice (+WC) as my trademark in their writings was appreciated by my students.

My favorite books for teaching included so many – Harper Lee's <u>To Kill a Mockingbird</u>, Mark Twain's <u>Huckleberry Finn</u>, and John Steinbeck's <u>Of Mice and Men</u> and <u>The Grapes of Wrath</u>. But I also enjoyed teaching <u>A Separate Peace</u>, <u>Lord of the Flies</u>, <u>The Chosen</u>, <u>The Crucible</u>, and <u>Brave New World</u> very much. Tackling <u>Crime and Punishment</u> with my one Advanced Placement English class was a healthy challenge. I was grateful for all the hard work my students and I put in when 69% of my AP students received college credit after passing the end of the year national tests. The next year when I was replaced by a team of two teachers, interestingly enough 43% of those students gained the college credit reward at the end of the course and test.

One semester a group of mothers offered to pray daily for one of my classes. From the looks of the class lists, I picked my third period class; it did not look very appealing. I was but shouldn't have been surprised when that class became my favorite after the faithful prayers of those moms. For me it was just another evidence that prayers work. Over my years of teaching at Lynden Christian I also turned to my friend Arv "Biffy Boy" Blankers for advice several times; he was very wise and helpful.

Unexpected joy came my way when an opening occurred with the retirement of teacher Marv Vander Pol. Since a teacher for the Speech classes was needed, I volunteered. Students shared so much of their lives in those classes, and I truly enjoyed teaching Speech more than any other class when all was said and done. One very shy student gave for his speech-to-persuade good reasons to get contact lenses rather than wear glasses for corrective eye care. After hearing Rob Visser's speech, I decided to lay aside my glasses of 15 years and move to contacts. I only needed a right eye contact lens, and my right eye has never regretted the change. My Speech course was capped off by what I called the 6-10 minute "chapelesque" speech, personal reflections of their learning at LC that would be fitting to share in a chapel. This effort dovetailed nicely later into the senior presentations that students were required to make.

When one of my students, another J. R., turned in his semester exam, he attached a sheet in fancy script and colors with what he deemed were "Mr. R's Pretty Wacky Expressions." Here are some from his list as he presented them: "Green weeney, bloney shooting, scum bucket, hokey smokey, wooley little bugger, a mind like a vise grip, and lots of jack in his back pocket." The always smiling Jordan Roorda and I shared some common initials but also some slang, I guess. More importantly, Jordan's family took in Rafael Siebenscheim, an exchange student from Switzerland. One of his parents was a nominal Jew and the other an atheist. After one year at LCHS Rafael returned to his homeland. After two weeks there he accepted Jesus Christ as his personal Savior, and he requested from chaplain Donna Vander Griend another year's learning at LC. In my class his special "chapelesque" speech was a prize and the best of the bunch. Even though he beat me up more than once on the tennis courts, I gladly gave him an A. Then he soared through Calvin. Later I had a delightful girl student named Prim Hangladoram, who came to LC from Thailand as a Buddhist but left LCHS as a believer also.

Another student holds a peculiar honor in my memory. At midterm, when endangered students were notified of their concerning grades, he was passing my course with a C- average, but he failed the last big test and the large writing project he did not complete so he earned an F for the quarter. That made him ineligible for playing in the soccer playoffs that fall. His parents were not pleased with me, but Brandon Rutledge said he got what he deserved and supported my decision for his grade and the consequence. Both so many regular students as well as some of the special exchange students added important pieces to my life.

My first two summers back in Lynden I worked for Farmers' Equipment, one summer outside repairing irrigation pipes and one inside building silage wagons. I needed to be outside after being cramped up in school for so many months. From 1980 and for 34 summers I painted houses to support my teaching habit. The wooden horses on which I laid my 16' plank came originally from a long gone LCS principal Ed Compaan. Working first with Judd Rinsema and Bill Brouwer, and later with Arv Blankers, for multiple summers led to lots of good experiences and stories. For one, I remember us painting the Fairhaven monstrosity of John and sister "Pooky." Our ladders reached about 35' up, but the top of the fourth floor was just not reachable to paint that way. So on the roof we tied a rope around Judd's waist, and he leaned over the edge to paint the face boards as his young son on the ground directed his painting while Bill and I hung tightly onto the rope wrapped around the chimney to secure our partner. Fortunately

Judd was virtually fearless and Bill and the rope were strong. We got the job done.

Around the painting work, camping offered welcomed relief for our family vacation over the family-rearing years. Many summers found the Blankers and Rozebooms with their tent trailers soaking up the sun in toasty Penticton, British Columbia. While I taught and coached, Jeannie worked at a clothing store called the New Crescent, ran the computer at the Cedar Springs resort in the foothills to the east, and then finished up with a lengthy hitch of 14 years as the well appreciated office manager for the Lynden Chamber of Commerce.

In the 2006 spring I made plans to begin the following fall in retirement. After 42 years of assignments and bells and lots of good days, I found I could say goodbye to the classroom at age 64 and a half. At graduation I used track analogies in my commencement speech to challenge graduates in their race for the prize of life.

On behalf of LCHS, then superintendent Don Kok and high school principal Keith Lambert presented me with an unexpected gift. It was a paid trip for me to go to Cooperstown, New York and visit major league baseball's Hall of Fame. What a surprising and gracious gift that was!

When Mom had some of my grade school and high school teachers come to our farm for a meal, I now can see how I was becoming aware of them as human beings. One meal was for Gord "Sarge" DeYoung and John VanderVeen, both confirmed bachelors "then." Later I would teach at SCHS with my HS math teacher John (called "Chief" at LCHS and "Smiley" at SCHS) Verstraete as well as John VanderVeen.

I learned a lot from a vast variety of students and colleagues in those 42 years of high school teaching. But I think sometimes I was a slow learner.

Having reached the third base of my life, the formal end of my work career and a long stretch, I took a deep breath and begin to consider some other things God might have in store for me.

24

Friday, the 13th

One fine Friday the 13th in October of 2002 I remember as my favorite day with teaching and officiating memories combined. It was, after all, a bright sunny day as I recalled my first date, engagement 37 years before, and marriage to Jeannie as I drove to school. Teachers at LCHS were expected to do something patriotic around devotions on Fridays at that time. In my first hour class we sometimes said the pledge of allegiance, or I played a recording of the national anthem. On this special day I said I'd be glad to sing the national anthem, if only I could. A big strapping basketball player named Paul Hafford, whose three-point bombs set records in Yakima at the basketball tournament, raised his hand and asked how much it would be worth if he sang it. "Ten points extra credit," I said. His acapella rendition was awe-inspiring and was met with a standing ovation from the class just like Cory Bergman, a swimmer of some renown, experienced the next week as he played the national anthem with his sax. That October Friday the 13th I walked on water at school.

After school I did my usual Friday night thing for 30 autumns – football officiating. Over that span of falls I officiated with 147 different crew mates, a rich variety. As usual I left Lynden around 4:00 p.m. and did not return till about midnight. That night in a football game, later called "the Possum Bowl" at Mt. Vernon High School, the lights went out in the second half; the crew led by "white

70

hat' Monte Walton agreed to return the next day. We learned a possum had crawled into the fuse box and arced out the lights. The next morning an electrician claimed he threw the possum out of the fuse box onto the ground where it shockingly walked away despite blowing a 6" hole in the fuse box. An interception ended that tight Saturday-ending game as the hometown Bulldogs beat the Seahawks of Anacortes. The interesting combination of memories and events made that Friday plus remarkable.

25

Clutch Hitting

On a sunny August afternoon at Sehome High School the score was tied - Aztecs 4 and Nationals 4 in the bottom of the ninth. On the hill cocky stringbean Ned Betts grimaced. With two outs and baserunners at 2B and 3B, the righthanded batter Jeff Morrison in the five-hole stepped up to the plate. The righty Ned checked the baserunners while Jeff took a practice cut. On deck #13 applied pine tar, stretched, and watched. From the stretch Ned uncorked a high inside pitch. It nicked Jeff's jersey. Now the bases were jammed as a lefty swinger stepped up to the plate. The outfielders moved in. Ned wound up and missed with a fastball low and away; the count became 1-0. Once more the baserunners took their leads. Once more Ned fired, this time it was a breaking ball down and away. #13, the lefty swinger, poked a soft drive just in front of the charging left fielder who dove and just missed a sensational shoestring catch. The winning run scored. The adult recreation league teammates raced to 1B and nearly crushed #13, who at age 64, had probably his only walk-off base hit in his lifetime. One week later against the same opposing team and in the top of the ninth at Joe Martin Stadium #13 hit what would become a game-winning drive over the drawn in right-fielder (6'6" Steve Chapman) as teammate Jeff scored again.

When I, the old #13, retired from playing adult league baseball, some joyful memories remain. They include a home run to right field just over the fence in Deming, one five-hit game against a team from Arlington, and two line drive hits, one through the 3-hole and one through the 6-hole against an upper 80's mph pitcher with a patch over his right eye. There was so much else in my playing to keep me humble, but I was thankful for the ride. For a decade Jacob Ferry led the way as the "guts and glue" guy of our team that achieved a lot of success in league play and tournaments. Lots of games, good people to play with and against, and fun.

26

Losing Mom and Dad

Laying Mom (age 87) and Dad (age 96) to rest after November 30, 2007 and on December 29, 2012 (on Mom's birthday) made for some somber reflection. But our family recalled with much joy their significant influences in the lives of family members as well as many others. Mom had Dad's support and help right up to the end of her life where they lived in their Lynden home together; congestive heart failure finally took her. Boxes and albums of pictures with written details on the back and artwork galore were part of her legacy. She painted with oils, chalk, and tints. My favorite was her tinted picture of our three little kids sitting by the sidewalk. Today her paintings of the homes of Dad and Mom on a milk can grace our sunroom. At their funerals Pastor Ben De Regt skillfully wove Ps. 27 and Ps. 130 into the celebrations of the lives of Mom and Dad respectively.

A story from when my mom was a little girl has stayed with me. Mom had accompanied her dad to get groceries one day. Much of the food could be found in barrels then. When Mom got home with lots of pink around her lips, her mom asked where the pink had come from. With pink cheeks no doubt, my mom said she had taken just one peppermint out of a barrel at the grocery store. Mom was taken back to the grocery store to confess her theft and offer restitution. Now I can picture Mom in heaven working in a beautiful garden or painting a beautiful picture and maybe sucking on a pink peppermint too. She had a green thumb, and art was in her. My sister said Mom had "elegant simplicity."

After a nasty bout with pneumonia and then a post-hip surgery stroke soon after that really curtailed his ability to talk, Dad spent his last three years in the Christian Health Care Center in Lynden. Almost every day when I came to see him, he was reading his Bible. I sang to and/or with him "Precious Lord, Take My Hand" every day for his last two years. Those two years were precious but also difficult. Writing a brief memoir of his life with his rich input before his stroke inspired me to try to do something similar for my heirs.

My favorite story from Dad's youth comes from his country swimming days. One summer day Uncle Bill and Dad were skinny dipping along with Hanky DeGroot in a creek on Casey DeGroot's farm. Casey had a goat that tagged along with the boys to the creek one day. On the banks of the creek the goat picked up the boys' clothes with its horns. Then it joined the boys in the water where their clothes were soaked. The unappreciative boys held the goat's head under water to teach it a good lesson. A problem ensued when the goat was under water too long and expired. The Rozeboom boys then trudged home to tell their dad about the drowning of the goat. They were sent to apologize to Casey and offer restitution for the goat. Casey said he didn't even like that old goat. The Rozeboom brothers had experienced a lesson in accountability but were grateful for Casey DeGroot's graciousness.

I still think of my dad who had no slick manners but was a gentleman from head to toe. He was very strong inside. Unless he was on a trip to visit our Minnesota kin, he never missed a milking; I saw him handle the flu by throwing up in the gutter and keep on milking. As I recall, his most common filler words were "By Corky" and "By Gravy." I never wanted to disappoint my dad, and I admired him so much. Dad had uncommon common sense and showed grace to everyone.

Like a two-horse hitch my parents worked well together. They taught me so much. They modeled commitment and faithfulness in their 66 years of marriage. I can hardly believe it, but I never heard them fight. I learned how important appreciating God's creation was even at sunrise when my dad and I had a cup of tea with graham crackers before tackling the chores in the barn. When Dad was 89 and Mom 86, they started lifting weights regularly as the equipment became available at the Lynden Community Senior Center. A fellow church member called them, "the pillars of the church." Both of my parents were blessed with many years of good health for the long haul of nearly nine decades each. They prized the many blessings of life. As time moves on, my appreciation for them grows more and more.

27

Whose Your Daddy?

Other people called my father "George." Like lots of little boys do, I followed Daddy around. He was tall, he seemed so big, and his stride was long. His imprint on my life has been clear. I never heard my dad say a negative word about anyone; I never heard him show disrespect to my mom. Without sophistication he was a gentleman. He practiced what he preached: "Moderation in all things;" he was so even keeled. He worked hard, but not too obsessively. He never gulped too much water when we were haying. He never drove too fast on the highway. When I was a kid, I thought he was strict as a parent, but as an adult now myself, I appreciate how he handled me as a kid. He was never confrontational. He never gave me easy victories in checkers; I had to earn a win, not be given one.

Dad had great internal strength. When things were financially tough on the farm, I never saw him get distraught or angry. I don't remember seeing tears in his eyes till Mom died. He was raised to be more comfortable with a handshake than a hug. Smiles and joy dominated his life in retirement. He knew he belonged to God; he memorized Heidelberg Catechism question and answer #1. He loved his Bible and faithfully read it for his spiritual nourishment. It's fair to say he had the Rozeboom tilt, a slightly forward bend at the hips. At the Senior Center the pool room provided him enjoyment every Thursday morning for years; his cronies sometimes referred to his "Minnesota magic" after crafty pool shots. When he was in his 90's, he still attended my adult league baseball games. Jeannie found him on the hillside sitting in a chair behind the backstop one day when she came to a game. "What did you do today, Dad?" she asked. His response heard by others sitting nearby was a surprise. "I memorized Ps. 130." And then he recited its six verses which included "Waiting on the Lord" as some ball game fans got a surprise.

When Dad was middle-aged, I wrote a description of him for a class at Morgan State University in Baltimore. The following is what I wrote. "Dad is no John Wayne, Charles Atlas, or Bob Richards. Physically Dad is a dandy specimen of health. Viewing Dad walking, one, at a distance, would readily be impressed by his even, purposeful stride, never too hurried or anxious. At this distance one would discover a figure of attractive manliness; his dress would never be too stylish, nor too fancy, nor too shabby, but he would always be simply attired. The observer would likely notice a restrained dignity, nearly an easy grace, in Dad's bearing. Nearer, Dad would reveal more of his fifty-one-year old physique. The kindly smile would seem to be stamped upon his lips. These lips would lie in the midst of a cleanshaven face, one well-tanned but not wrinkled. A rather healthy nose divides his clear and twinkling blue eyes. Just a few specks of white are beginning to cloud his generally dark brown sideburns. Further down, at either side of Dad's muscular torso, a pair of strong arms with farmer veins leads to two large, nearly overdeveloped hands. His greeting can be felt before it is heard.

Without doubt, this physically fit man enjoys work and play. After five decades of challenging rural work, Dad has not lost his love of contest. He will still give his twelve-year old son Ric a short "run for the money" foot race. Although he lacks the ruggedness of John Wayne, the muscle of Charles Atlas, and the peak athletic fitness of Bob Richards, his physical strength is complemented by a gentleness of spirit.

Someone has said, "A man's life is an open book." That Dad is gentle and kind has been witnessed by many members of the community in which he lives. His humble life of ready service before sometimes severe and unjust judges has produced only respectful and laudatory responses. He has positively influenced some very unmanageable and irascible people around him. No one need feel uneasy in his presence.

Another has said, "Home is where the hurt is." In Dad's home there has never been much of an ill atmosphere. Assisted by his matchless mate, Dad with practical wisdom and gentle direction has helped to produce a stable home. In Dad's discipline of his four children his impact has primarily been felt rather than heard. He has gently dismissed his own burdens, hurts, and anxieties from the rest of the family.

The Bible says, "Out of the heart are the issues of life." (Prov. 4:23 in NIV) Because Dad's heart and beliefs are centered in a strong faith in God, his life has reflected and asserted the spirit of Christianity. In a spirit of gentleness he has not given principle over to practicality.

That Dad isn't financially rich nor physically powerful doesn't mean much; he is an aristocrat in gentleness." When I wrote that description of him, Dad was 51 years old.

The role of a father is a significant one. How a man treats his wife and children says a lot. A father with an attitude of gratitude helps his children to look at life positively. How he works, neither obsessively nor lazily, is a great example for his heirs. What he treasures tells what's in his heart. A good earthly father makes it easier for his children to believe in their Heavenly Father.

28

Sibs

After many a day of grade school, I'd come home and take out my frustrations on my little sister. Some people referred to "Pooky" as a Shirley Temple with her flowing locks. Two years younger than I, my sister Ida became my friend when we were in high school; she helped me out in countless ways but especially in the social realm. "Pooky" and her husband John were high school sweethearts and both graduated from Calvin College. "Moley" served in the military before earning his law degree and working many years for U.S. Department of Housing and Urban Development while Ida was a social worker and an interior designer. They have called several Pacific Northwest geographic locations their home. They were blessed with two children - John, who married Valerie and they have three little boys, and daughter Jacki. Jacki and husband Jonathan Houghten live in Austin, Texas while all the VanderMolens now live in Bellingham.

1950 brought a nasty snowstorm in January and then in September my happy little brother Gerry. One neighbor called him "Tex" because he was a little bowlegged. Early on he showed his interest in parts. After he spent his adult working career as the parts manager at Berger Chevrolet in Grand Rapids, I recall a time when Dad and I did the chores and Gerry, about five years old, was nowhere in sight. When we all came in the house, Mom wanted to wash his clothes; she found a big bunch of fastener nuts in the pockets of Gerry's pants. He had taken them off Dad's side delivery rake while we milked. Furthermore his interest in music, both on the trumpet and with his voice, has led to blessings for others. On one Calvin College choir trip Ger met his future wife, Liz. That Engelhard girl was talented in many ways, and together they produced three daughters - Becky, Bethany, and Melissa, who have joyfully given Ger and Liz eight grandchildren, some living in Washington and some in Grand Rapids, Michigan.

Brother Eric arrived in 1955. Since his brother was called "Tex," he nicknamed himself "Cactus." With 13 years separating Ric and me, he was the little brother Ricky that I played with when I came home from college each summer; he really like to play ball with me. After high school Ric married Sharon Van Beek; from their marriage came two daughters – Tonya and Leesha – and so far two grandchildren. Ric's skill as an excellent welder and handyman was pretty widely known. The curse of his alcohol addiction led to a loss of jobs and a breakdown of his marriage and family. He spent his last good years serving as a maintenance manager for a Bible camp in Southwest Washington. In March of 2016 we learned he had lost his life trying to self-detox hoping for a new start. The family's comfort rested on his profession of faith cousin Loren Rozeboom from Idaho heard at my dad's funeral.

For me schooling two younger brothers was fun though rather shortly experienced because of our age differences. Each one of my siblings has added something very special to my life. Whenever we three still living siblings get together, we have precious times.

29

Heirs

More than a few years ago, our three children were little ones. And now they are all "growed up." Being present in the room at Kara's birth was something I was talked into by friends. Seeing the miracle of her being born was an awesome experience indeed. When Paul, age 5, was bitten in the cheek by a dog on my parents' farm, Jeannie and I experienced an overwhelming desire to take his pain away. The bite led to some 60 stitches and scars that today help us prize him even more. One miracle was that the bite did not go into his salivary glands. The very competitive Dave loves playing games of all kinds. For our young family Sunday afternoon was always game time.

After stints of college administration in Texas at Baylor University, St. Edwards University in Austin, and Hardin-Simmons University in Abilene, Dave, known as Dr. Boom, has moved to North Carolina where he is serving as the vice-president of student development at Mars Hill University to use some of his Ph.D. knowledge gathered at Texas A+M earlier. And, yes, he proudly wears a big Aggie ring. The children of Dave and Deena, a teacher before the kids came and sometimes substitute and an elementary teacher, are a HSU senior Drew ("Champ") and Baylor University sophomore Dani ("Princess") and maturing grade schoolers Desi ("Oppie" in 8th grade) and Dakota ("Tootsie" in 6th grade); both love playing games of all kinds. Many new pets have replaced the dog Deuce in the "D" home. Just as lots of high school students and athletes and cars received nicknames, Papa just had to give a pet name to each of his grand kids.

Paul and Sue have made their home in Grand Rapids, Michigan. It lies between their places of employment – Paul, who has evolved from an electrical engineer into his architectural and engineering company's treasurer, works out of his offices in Lansing and Grand Rapids while Sue uses her education at Calvin Seminary, her Ph.D. from Notre Dame, and her ordination in the CRC to teach Western Seminary students in Holland, MI. Their two maturing youngsters are Liesl ("Lady" in 9th grade) and Annemarie ("Lassie" in 7th grade); ballet and music have helped to produce two very balanced and creative individuals.

At Kara's wedding, she and I danced together to "Butterfly Kisses," a special thrill for me; it matched witnessing her birth. Today Kara and Josh Gillanders, her Mr. Right, live in Edmonds, just north of Seattle. Josh has moved into a career in physical therapy after years in maritime work, lastly as a shipping agent. Kara has used her Masters' degree to serve in different areas of social work, presently as a lecturer and field instructor for Eastern Washington University. The growing little ones of Josh and Kara are Kenzie ("Kitten" age 7), a second grader, and Caden ("Dookie" age 5), starting kindergarten. Papa (me) and Nana (Jeannie) find much joy in watching these grands growing weekly. The little ones like to playfully mock us with "Papa jalopa" and "Nana banana." Each Thursday we have seen them; Fridays, and sometimes Saturdays, are good for recovery time. With both of them in school in the '19 fall our Thursdays are different.

So many times Jeannie and I have read Ps. 127 and Ps. 128 with gratitude for the gift of our heirs' lives. We stand amazed at how the Lord brought a Jeannie from California and a John from Washington to meet in Michigan at Calvin College (now University) and how their three children all graduated also from

Calvin before going their own ways. We pray every day for our sons and daughter and their mates and for their children and what they are becoming. We're eager to see how God will use the giftedness of each one in His kingdom.

30

Retirement Goals

I have found retirement to be a pretty busy time after all. I had set several goals in 2006 June. One was doing a lot more reading; that's been easy. After 12 years of retirement I have read 199 books. Five of my goals have reasonably been achieved; but the goals of teaching myself to play an organ we had and learning how to play golf decently I have easily relinquished. I am fine with that. And I pretty much quit playing in league recreational basketball games when I turned 70 mostly due to lack of players at the YMCA on their noon breaks. Due to physical deterioration in my arm and legs I quit playing baseball regularly at age 71. Now my main sport is tennis, an almost every summer Tuesday evening activity I enjoy.

Starting at age 60 in 2002, I got a new lease in my recreational life. Fastpitch softball had been a steady summer diet for most of my life, but in 2002 I started playing adult baseball and did so for 12 years besides serving as the "commish" for the then BBL (Borderline Baseball League) for the final six years. At age 69 I managed to nail a pair of 88 mph fastballs for base hits in one memorable game.

In the 2007 summer Jeannie and I traveled with our friends, Don and Marcia Steeby, to visit major league baseball's Hall of Fame in Cooperstown, New York. How fun to see games at historic Fenway - where we sat very near the Pesky pole, old Yankee

Stadium with its monuments, and Detroit's Comerica Park. Those were unique experiences.

Our seats in deep right field at Fenway Park were a pricey $68 apiece. It's interesting to note that the Orioles' first batter hit the first pitch of the game into the right field seats for a home run not too far from us. But we all missed seeing it as a gal with shapely legs and high heels was carrying a tray of beers up the steep incline to her friends sitting a few rows in front of us. We couldn't believe her balance. Then the next day at Yankee Stadium we got a special deal for seniors at $5 a seat, and we were even closer to the action.

Since my retirement Jeannie and I have visited Phoenix, Arizona where half of the major league baseball teams do spring training. We both thoroughly enjoy watching Mariner and Dodger games while getting our blood warmed up for a couple weeks in the "Valley of the Sun" at the Cactus League games each March. Believe it or not, Jeannie is the one who has insisted on this annual trip and time together. She became a baseball convert when she, like so many ladies in the Pacific Northwest, saw Joey Cora crying in the dugout after a 1995 elimination game for the Mariners. Before that she spent most of the time socializing at games I played in or coached.

In the rides down from and back up to Washington, the evergreen state, we have marveled at the beauty of many locales in the West, especially in Utah with its awesome natural parks.

Our latest family reunion was this past June of 2019 in Scottsdale, AZ. Seventeen of us gathered for a week at a resort to celebrate family and growth. Grandson Drew took his girlfriend Crissy Haden on an exhausting mountain hike so she would agree to marry him. It worked. Seeing a growing and often glowing family is such a delight for Jeannie and me. Having a close-knit family is a rich blessing.

31

How Are You Feeling?

I guess as a kid I didn't think I'd ever get to be a teenager, much less 21 years old and older. People in their 40's seemed old and those in their 60's ancient nearly. My life has been largely free of health setbacks. My only bone break occurred when I was a senior in college and playing in an alumni basketball game at LC one Christmas. I learned no mat had been mounted on the north wall of the gym after I plunged my left wrist through the wall after flying through the air and trying to block a shot. Looking at my wrist, Coach Timmer declared, "It's broken," and he was right. Playing lots of ball games has helped keep me in pretty good shape.

When I was 30 years old, I pledged to run two miles or do an equivalent activity that was strenuous every other day. I did that till last fall when I was nearly 76 when my right hip started aching. I needed help with my vision at age 30 and with my hearing a couple years ago. I smoked my last cigarette, a Tareyton given me by Curt Brink, our SCHS shop teacher, on a date I chose so I could remember it easily – 11.7.77 – to kick an 18-year bad habit. I had three hernia repair jobs by one Dr. VanderGriend or another starting in the 1990's. In 2015 the pain in my right shoulder led to a rotator cuff surgery; I had hoped for a bionic arm after it but no; that was just a pipe dream. I guess throwing about an hour of baseball practice every spring for 40 years took its toll on my right arm and right hip.

I likely played my last recreational basketball game on a team led by Shane Bajema one Saturday morning in '17 December when I was 75; years earlier I had played with his dad Cliff in HS and also one Saturday morning with a young hotshot sixth grader, Shane's son Cole. I finished the game by sinking four of my five shots attempts, four from the outside; that was better than my usual percentage. Limping since playing in that basketball game, I received a right hip joint replacement the '18 fall. My surgeon was Dr. Joel Hoekema, who 35 years earlier was the cerebral center of the offensive line on my football team at Lynden Christian. I might no longer get to do some high impact activities. I thought earlier I would be able to jog again; now I may have to bike instead; we'll see.

Starting about a decade ago, I have had my skin checked twice annually; I had a piece of my left shoulder removed because of melanoma concerns a couple years ago. Wear and tear is part of my story, and I am reminded of my mortality as well as the blessing that good physical health is.

In 1987 Jeannie stepped off a piece of plywood in the attic and fell through the particle board 12' to the garage cement floor beneath. She only broke her heel which has nicely healed. While incapacitated, she received from our church family so many wonderful banana breads and more. Then in 2012 her need for a triple-by-pass surgery was a shock. From that, too, she rebounded nicely and even ran a 5-K less than a year later. The second half of 2017 was a very difficult time for her; we now think it was viral labyrinthitis. We read Psalm 130 lots of times and were carried on the wings of others' prayers. Jeannie was diagnosed in that summer with chronic subjective dizziness, a special kind of acid reflux, and scarring of the lungs. In that December she also learned she has Parkinson's. However, she has been functioning normally much of the time since the beginning of 2018 in what she calls her "new normal." Exercise and diet changes have helped. With all she has endured and is enduring, she has been a trooper.

Daughter-in-law Sue and family had to deal with her serious

bout with Hodgkin's, but gratefully she is over that trial. Daughter-in-law Deena is coping with CODP with monthly infusions. We know that good health is a huge gift. We also know that there are all kinds of health – physical yes, but also mental, emotional, and spiritual wellbeing.

We pray our heirs will understand their value of self as being a child of the King, not from their intelligence, physical looks, or bank account or as I paraphrase Dr. Dobson's view of the big three of American values for self-worth - "Beauty, brains, and bucks."

We look to God daily for His grace in our lives, our kin's lives, and our friends' lives. We know the "music" of organ recitals is not always beautiful. We don't know what the future holds, but we do know Who holds the future. And we rest in the promise of Jeremiah 29:11.

32

Volunteering

So much has been given us, and now we have ample opportunity to give to others. Why would anyone ever be bored later in life?

Tucked into our schedules these last few years have been service trips for World Renew's Disaster Relief Services; Jeannie and I have served in needs assessment for flood victims in Colorado in early 2014, fire victims in Central WA in late 2014, fire victims in Northern California in early 2016, flood victims in Baton Rouge in early 2017, and Hurricane Irma victims in Orlando, Florida in the 2018 summer. Interviewing lots of people in these two-week stints has been emotionally and physically draining, but rewarding when we believe the local long range recovery group in each place will get many more resources beyond FEMA's first shot in the arm for some to help the yet very needy. We're abundantly thankful that our church's denomination has created this niche that becomes part of the ears, hands, and feet of Christ. Having Harry and Phyllis Kuiper, some of my first students at SCHS, as supervisors has been a very special arrangement and treat twice.

My life in recent years revolves around a lovely schedule. For the last couple years each Monday I spend an hour with a needy student at Lynden Public School as part of the Be-the-One Mentorship program. Friend Herm Fransen inspired me to take on this challenge. Tuesday morning is Men's Prayer and Share time at a local café. What a blessing to be a part of a group of veteran Christians who can still share joys and sorrows. Named the "Vintage Group," we support needy seminary students. We also hitch up with the high school age boys of our church so we can pray daily for them. Often on Tuesday evenings I have provided a ride to and from an AA meeting for men from Bridges of Hope, a halfway house for former inmates. Each Wednesday is my opportunity to help out the meals-on-wheels program locally; I deliver each meal with a little verse. That's after a visit to Senior Men's coffee with an apple fritter at church. Each week I receive from an inmate a Bible lesson via Crossroad Prison Ministries. I am asked to correct the objective questions and read all the essay responses and then write the inmate a one-page letter of encouragement. So many of these inmates wrestle with grace and forgiveness in their lives. My heart breaks for them.

Thursday has been a bonding date for the last seven years; Jeannie and I have driven the 93 miles to babysit in Edmonds our grandkids Kenzie and Caden. Thursdays have been big days but precious days for us. Regularly at mid-morning we used to tuck them into their strollers and push them a two-mile jaunt to Starbuck's for a "Nana treat." The snack for Kenzie used to be some bites of Nana's morning bun and for Caden bites of Papa's classic coffee cake. That was then, but this is the latest: they each favor their own pastry picks – chocolate croissant now is a popular choice. Now a second grader, Kenzie can only join us when she doesn't have a school day and Caden is in kindergarten. After the morning's excursion and lunch came naps. After some nap time singing by Papa in the early afternoon, both now know "Take me out to the ball game" versions for both the Mariners, Nana's first baseball love, and the Dodgers, Papa's first baseball love.

Not exactly is it volunteering, but serving as a member of our church's council and in the education program has taken up lots of time also. Unfortunately serving a double hitch as the council and elder chair at church (2014-2016) brought more than a light load of duty. In my first 365 days as council and elder chair I attended and often led 100 meetings, often dealing with some significant staff adjustments and concerns after many families had left our church. A couple caring elders really stood by my side and lightened my load of leadership. I was thankful, too, for the many folks of our church that offered their support during a difficult juncture that required so much difficult confidentiality from the elders. But Third Church is in an upturn mode since the positive contributions of specialized transitional minister Les Kuiper from the twin cities area of Minnesota as well as new initiatives from the ministry teams. Bared in some ways but surely spared, Third Church is hoping to experience rejuvenation with Pastor Jon Young, who started his ministry at Third Church the fall of 2016, and a renewal team. The future is hopeful. And I know "the church" is all believers everywhere and from all times, and I have learned we all need loads of grace.

During my week of synod at Dordt College in Sioux Center, Iowa in mid-June of 2015 I experienced the power of the Holy Spirit bringing divergent groups to consensus on various issues. As a kid I thought church was a sanctuary for the saints, well dressed as they were; now I know the church is a hospital for the needy, including me. Every Easter every person of the congregation that wants to come up front to join in the singing of the "Hallelujah" chorus of the "Messiah" may do so. I'm thrilled to participate in that rendition every spring. I long for eternity when there will be no divisions and all tribes and nations will experience rich diversity and wonderful unity as true teammates.

33

What Old Geezers Can Do

In Arizona the Los Angeles Dodgers held a baseball fantasy camp for a week in 2015 January; I was 73 years old then. A few years before I had enjoyed participating in a couple of three-day fantasy baseball camps directed by the Tacoma Rainiers and Hendu (Dave Henderson). But in Tucson, my high school teammate Arlen De Young from 1960 and I played baseball every day surrounded by 15 former major leaguers and/or present coaches.

Having a locker next to catcher Steve Yeager (famous for the chin flap protector) and centerfielder Rick Monday (famous for stamping out a protester's burning flag in the outfield once during a game) and being coached by Bill Russell (who has played more games than any other Dodger in history) of the '81 World Series champion Dodgers was interesting, to say the least. Getting a compliment from one-time batting champ Tommy Davis for the defensive play of the game for a pick I made at 1B was an honor. Just barely scoring from 3B after a wild pitch and chugging to home plate with a bent leg slide, I only heard from Rick Monday, "Why didn't you go wide open?" At that night's banquet a video had to show that play over and over as the "play of the day." Going to that camp was a bucket list item that became a reality for me!

My last baseball experiences so far have been playing in the June LCHS baseball alumni games of 2016 and 2017. Getting a base hit as a 74- year old off the Lyncs' high school varsity closer in 2016, playing some lB, and playing on an alumni team with so many of my players of the past was very rewarding. To see several of my former football and baseball players at LCHS as coaches at LC right now is gratifying. I have enjoyed a wonderful network of connections by being involved in sports.

34

Major Learning

The main thing I have learned is how delicate and precious life is. Together on our journey, Jeannie, my matchless mate, and I were able to celebrate in Palm Springs in the 2015 summer our 50th wedding anniversary with all our treasured heirs. We did it again this past summer (2019) in Scottsdale. There I did learn how important it is to stay on the trail on our Camelback hike. To be altogether as a family coming from WA, MI, and TX for one week in one place is really wonderful. We'd done that earlier in 2002 in Escondido, California and in 2010 in Texas near where Dave's family lived.

One way to see how time marches on is to see the changing role of media. I relished reading the newspaper daily from childhood till this past fall. But with my cell phone coverage of news and stories this fall I put to rest our two newspapers – the shrinking Bellingham Herald and the U.S.A. Today. A few years ago this would've been hard to imagine. We keep adjusting. With all the social media we pray our heirs will learn to be discriminating.

One major bit of learning over the years has been seeing the twin enemies to truth often raise their ugly heads – rationalization and denial. Our thinking can really get clouded. I think really important words to use are "please," "thank you," and "I'm sorry" (good manners Nana calls them). My favorite words of the English language are "belong" and "reconcile." These words are loaded with spiritual implications. Being saved is eternal life insurance; but to yield every part of my life to the lordship of Christ has been a long process. To be "perceptive, caring, and transformational," LC's motto, has reminded me for years of my goal as a husband, father, teacher, elder, coach, and ball player. I want to live on the bedrock of faith no matter what the changing circumstances are. I hope that for our children and our grandchildren as well as for all my former students. I anticipate the touching of the eternal home plate. I've made lots of mistakes. But to God be the glory for great things He has done for, in, and sometimes even through me. The bottom line is "Amazing Grace" – **G**od's **r**iches **at** **C**hrist's **e**xpense. Without His grace I know I'm "dead meat," or as son-in-law Josh would say, "chopped liver."

35

Looking Ahead

Who knows what my "Snooky" and I may yet do. Lord willing, it's a good bet that we will continue with volunteering – I doing my weekly Bible lesson and write letter of encouragement for a prison inmate via PMI (Prison Ministries International) and delivering in Husky, my '95 Chevy truck, meals-on-wheels along with a verse. The fall of 2016 I began to mentor a Lynden High School freshman who came from a clearly dysfunctional home and was flunking most of his courses; now he has his GED. Now I have a 8th grader to mentor. Daily Scrabble and Hooked on Words games and reading will hopefully keep my mind active. And listening to Southern Gospel music delights my soul. Meanwhile Jeannie, besides lots of social interaction, volunteers at the hospital in Bellingham in part as well as serving as a shepherd at church and a cashier at LC's Second Chance store. Spending a part of most mornings at the Homestead Fitness Center gets Jeannie and me going. Keeping in touch with loved ones a long way away is a top priority. We had prayed for our children, "Lord, use them as You wish." He has, and they are planted and being used as transforming agents in three different states. And, of course, we'll follow our special teams as we anticipate our final homecoming.

Part II

My Life Inside Coaching

36

Looking Back at Coaching Memories

An Introduction

On my life's trip around the bases I am definitely past third base and on the way to home. Having lived over three quarters of a century, I have done some reflecting on my past. Since coaching has played a significant role within my life's journey, I have been challenged to share some of that.

I spent 40 years investing in high school student athletes. There were definite ups and downs with my teams and coaching, but through it all I met many fine young men at Grand Rapids (MI) South Christian, and Lynden (WA) Christian, two private high schools.

I have lots of positive memories of my coaching time at South Christian after spending 14 years there. For me there were so many firsts and so many fine athletes there. Then I moved from the Midwest to the West Coast for 28 years at Lynden Christian. Some of my very fine LC baseball teams garnered three league titles in the mid- '90's. Over an 11-year span from the 1993 season on, LC was the only team in the county to earn a post-season berth every year. After 21 years as the baseball head coach at LC, I retired. In the fall of that same 2006-year, statewide baseball coaching colleagues inducted me into the WA State HS Baseball Association's Hall of Fame; a dozen former players, assistant coaches, and my parents made the 100-mile trip to Seattle for the ceremony. This honor is now nicely symbolized for my players and myself with the Hall of Fame ring I wear and with my name on a plaque at the Seattle Mariners' newly renamed T-Mobile Park. Every player I ever coached has contributed to my ring. Coaching the two school baseball varsities to almost 400 wins was satisfying, but a lot of learning for me and for my players came from the losses.

I have concluded that good players make coaches look good. Two of my baseball players signed pro contracts; Walt Faber '78 of SCHS and Jon Vander Griend '91 of LCHS played professionally three years in the chain of the Tigers and Angels respectively after productive collegiate careers at Western Michigan University and the University of Washington. That southpaw pitcher and that southpaw hitter were certainly outstanding high school and beyond players. But the bottom line is this: what kind of men all my former players became is so much more important to me than what they accomplished on the gridiron or the diamond.

Being raised on a farm near the foothills of the Cascade Mountains in the northwest corner of the state of Washington, I learned lots about work and responsibility as well as balancing that out with play. That has blessed me. As a kid I partly lived in a sports' fantasy world. I created my own fictional high school with its football, basketball, and baseball teams; each team had some athletes that I created – like quick little lefty Chuck Evans and big brawny Buck Brill. For example, in football Evans would pass to Brill (Chuck to Buck), and in hoops Evans was a guard and Brill a bruising forward.

Around the seventh grade I began to play and enjoy the real games of school and summer teams. Playing high school basketball and baseball for Lynden Christian High School, usually between 300 and 400 students and the A classification in Lynden, Washington provided me with a variety of very positive experiences. At division III Calvin College in Grand Rapids, Michigan I was blessed with the opportunity to play a year of college basketball and four years of baseball for the Knights. Making the conference all-star team in baseball as a senior was rewarding. Someone has said, "You don't grip the baseball; it grips you." That was becoming true for me. Yeah for baseball, hotdogs, apple pie, and Chevrolet – I love 'em all!

After college I continued playing recreational hoops and fastpitch and/or adult league baseball into my '70's. What follows are some of my memories of coaching and athletes I've met at two different, but quite similar high schools, where I always proudly wore the school colors of navy blue and white, and like the Dodgers' Tommy Lasorda, I bled blue. After I was inducted into the Washington State High School Baseball Coaches' Hall of Fame in 2006, the following spring LC gifted me with a trip to the MLB Hall of Fame in Cooperstown, New York upon my retirement from teaching. What a blessed surprise that was!

Playing baseball is a lot of life preparation. It takes lots of courage to step into the batter's box to face a pitcher, especially a hard thrower who is a bit wild. Sacrifices are important; they help the team. Players need to recover from lots of failures. Sometimes baseball, like life, is a grind which calls for lots of practice and perseverance.

Lots of rich opportunities have come to me as a person and as a coach. As a ballplayer, official, coach, and player besides, I can only be thankful for all the opportunities I have been given and for the support of Jeannie, my gracious wife. My Gram once said what Jeannie never would say, "Oh, you got another old ball game today?"

Coaching Memories at SCHS (South Christian High School) 1965-1978

After my years of playing college baseball and two seasons of serving as a high school volunteer assistant baseball coach for the veteran John Meindertsma at South Christian, I took one year off before I was given my first opportunity to lead the diamond Sailors.

1968, my first spring at the helm, revealed a rather bare cupboard (no returning starters from the year before, yet some great kids) with lots of eager sophomores in the grades 10-12 high school to build around; one player, Paul Theule, talked me into keeping and not cutting him; he became the team's winningest pitcher with four of the team's six wins; later for his career he served as a school administrator. A senior on my first team later became a valued coaching assistant and friend – Garry "Ringer" Ringnalda; as a player he used his ability to bunt and run to good advantage in baseball. For his career this positive guy ran an insurance agency.

"Ringer" recalls what happened in one game at Kenowa Hills. From 1B he attempted to steal 2B believing he'd seen the indicator and the steal sign from me. In that close game he was out stealing, and I replaced him in the line-up. He remembers me getting very upset by his stolen base attempt because I thought I had not given him the steal sign. After the game and back at school, I met with the team over the confusing base-running issue. I asked if anybody saw the steal sign that "Ringer" thought he saw. Paul Griffeth said, "You gave the sign, Coach." Then I apparently apologized to "Ringer" for my huff and to the team for my sloppy sign giving that led to an out. I was learning as a coach.

By **1970** the sophomores of '68 had become the seniors of '70 with lots of confidence and wins and fun. On that team was Billy "Bam Bam" VanderHaar. On one test in my English class he drew a stick figure wearing a football helmet; that figure was picking his nose. On the helmet it said "Green Bay Pickers" to mock my favorite pro team. In one game at Kenowa Hills "Bam Bam" made a big play; he nearly disappeared over a hill to retrieve a long drive to right field hit over his head into an apple orchard. His relay to 2B-man Bob Blacquiere was perfect as was the relay of "Blackie" to lB-man Marv Hofman as was the relay of southpaw "Marvelous" to home plate where young catcher Jerry "Piggy" Syswerda made the tag at home plate to wipe out any thought of an inside-the-park home run. Sometimes mischievous, "Bam Bam" did not graduate with his class, but within a year there he was, with Salem cigarettes tucked in his denim bib overall, knocking on my classroom door to proudly show me his GED. Some 20 years later I was living in Washington when I received a gratifying handwritten letter on yellow legal pad from him. "Bam Bam" has been a tavern owner and a trucker in his work world, and I understand "Piggy" spent lots of years working for Steelcase Manufacturing.

We had one special practice experience when Calvin College's vocal Coach Jim Czanko invited my high school team to practice with his college team. After some drills Coach Czanko divided up all the players for a scrimmage. The best moment I recall occurred when my righty pitcher Doug Kramer threw a screwball that Calvin's Doug Tjaatjes swung over for strike three.

The physically impressive Calvin baseball player took his bat and slammed it on home plate and snapped it in half. Coach "Czank" bellowed, "Tjaatjes, that'll be $25 from you to me tomorrow!" The 6'5" Tjaatjes had been a truly outstanding high school three-sport athlete from Raymond, Minnesota, and he was drafted by a National Football League team even though he had not played college football. He did excel in his college basketball playing for the Knights.

Winning the Michigan Christian School Invitational of eight teams behind the Doug "Dugger" Kramer and Gord "Gogo" Oeverman pitching combo put a feather in the 1970 team's cap. One weekend was memorable. In a Friday afternoon nonleague-game we beat Byron Center 13-12; the key play was a base-running mistake by an opponent player. With the bases loaded and one out late in the game, a Byron Center batter hit a deep fly to centerfield. Their 3B-runner immediately raced for home. However, our centerfielder

"Gogo" not only caught the ball for out #2 but fired a one-bounce throw to home to nail the too late tagging up runner for a double play that enabled us to come back later and gain the win. Then on Saturday we triumphed three times capped by beating East Grand Rapids Christian 15-6. Winning four games over a 25-hour span required a truly huge team effort. After high school Gord has worked in roofing and Doug in the construction business.

One of our trophies that '70 season was for second place in the Wyoming Invitational Tournament. In our 2-1 loss to the champion Rockford Rams, two things I recall: one, I had not prepared my battery mates well enough on how to execute a pitchout so one 3B Ram runner scored on a wild pitch that became a pitchout gone awry and the eventual winning run; and secondly, in the last inning we trailed by a run, as our leadoff batter made an out, our #2 batter sophomore Tommy "King" Ellens reached first base safely, and our #3 batter flied out to short centerfield; so with two outs I signaled Tommy to try steal 2B against the Rams' rocket-armed catcher. On the next pitch Tommy slid in head first as the throw from the Rams' catcher arrived just in time near second base to ricochet off Tommy's helmet into the leftfield alley; but Tommy was dazed and could just get up and only muster getting to 3B where he stayed as our #4 hitter popped out to end the game. Tom settled into real estate work after doing some teaching earlier.

In those years I had no L screen to protect my body during batting practice when batters were hitting. With tremendous wrist action Dick Norden, my slightly built cleanup hitter and SS, loved ripping liners up the middle past a very concerned coach. Ironically "Ripper" Norden never injured me with all his bullets through the mound area, but strangely enough another year or two later a player who did not get a hit all season caught a pitch just right and gave me a bruised shin that was black and blue for many months after.

With my idealism, I expected a lot from that special group of '70 seniors. During their senior spring all kinds of students were skipping school and getting away with it. One day we were to play Lee High School. I learned at noon that my 1B-man and my leftfielder were missing from school. My 1B-man's dad shared with me some useful information; my 1B-man, who was my #3 batter, had said something on the phone before school about already having his clubs in the trunk of his car. After both boys arrived at school for the afternoon classes, the principal pulled me into the office and told me they could not play in the game that day; he wanted to make an example of them. After my arbitration on their behalf with the principal and athletic director, the boys were permitted to play. After school I learned my #4 batter, who was my SS, had missed school all day to visit a sister and her new baby in Muskegon; he, too, was in trouble with the authorities. Before our team left to play Lee HS, I said we had to deal with an issue after the game. We won the away game 3-1. Back at school in the parking lot, I asked the naughty boys if they had anything to say to the team. My normally genial outfielder, Larry "Curses" Kerstetter, acted somewhat indignant, and none of the boys said anything. So I, with a crushed spirit, shoved sophomore Larry Zinger out of the way and uttered a barnyard expression as I entered the school door. I took a long, hot shower wondering what would follow. Well, one by one the three young men came to the coaches' office to apologize for letting the team down by not owning up to missing school. I slept well that night after all. My outfielder became a sheriff, my SS became an electrician, and my 1B-man became a pastor. The team's chicken dinner after the season was tasty.

Incidentally underclassman "Zing" may have been one of the toughest players I coached in my 40 years; as a football running back he played half a season with a broken bone in his lower leg, and as a baseball SS he once took a bad hop in the jewels and barely winced. Zing was pretty quiet but what a tough ballplayer he was! I have learned he worked for his dad's business before moving to Montana.

Bob "Blackie" Blacquiere, my junior varsity football QB and my 1968-1970 baseball team's 2B-man and leadoff batter, spent a lengthy career at SCHS as a history teacher and highly successful football coach; after leading and helping Sailor teams to a couple state championships, he was honored to be inducted in the Michigan State High School Football Coaches' Hall of Fame. A rare incident occurred on a golf course when "Blackie," then a young teacher and very good at history trivia, was protecting me in case of a stray golf ball drive while I was in a hole gluing some pcv pipe together as we worked for Flier Underground Sprinkling Systems one summer. About 90 feet away the golfer teed off. "Blackie" hollered, I ducked, and the errant ball brushed the top of my head where my temple had been when the lousy golfer made his swing. My former 2B-man had a big save that day! Maybe he should've been a pitcher too.

Predicted to finish low in the 10-team league, the **1972** Sailor team surprisingly won the school's first league championship. I was privileged to coach South Christian's first O.K. (Ottawa Kent) White Conference champs in baseball during the spring of '72 and in football during the fall of '73. Many gifted athletes blessed SCHS during that time. They certainly had to overcome some of my coaching inexperience. One big mistake I made was giving our catcher a sign suggesting our pitcher throw a third straight curve ball; Tom Moore, the #3 hitter of Rogers High School, had missed the first two breaking balls, but he drove the third one back into centerfield for the game-winning base hit. That pitch gave very effective sophomore pitcher, Brian "Yoyo" Ellens, his only loss in 13 decisions for his sophomore season. His three-year high school stats included an impressive 34-6 won-loss record, a 0.88 e.r.a., and 71% strikes in 280 IP. He went on to play college baseball and basketball for Calvin College before heading up a window washing business a few years ago.

As coach of the O.K. White Conference champs I was honored to coach the league all-stars in the John Bos All-Star Game. Our opponent in the '72 game was the City League all-stars. Our O.K. White Conference's coaches had selected 14 players as all-stars, but it was my option to add two more players for that big game. I chose a hard throwing, burly righthander from Rogers High School as an extra pitcher and from my own team Tom Ellens, a senior who was very versatile defensively and a fine bunter and baserunner despite a low batting average that year; a perfect utility man, he could also pitch. As our team entered the top of the ninth inning, we trailed 3-4. I brought in the Rogers' righty, who managed to create some drama by walking the bases full and then striking out the side. In the bottom of the ninth, David Coates, the tall, muscular senior 1B-man from Rogers and my #3 batter, blasted a one-out triple off the right field wall. Next up was my own sophomore Bill "Powerhouse" Blacquiere, who had experienced a tremendous year defensively and offensively for the Sailors. He slammed a game-tying triple also off the right field wall and stood at 3B as the potential winning run with one out. I decided to pinch hit Tom Ellens for the #5 batter. On the first pitch with "Powerhouse" racing home, Tom dropped a perfectly executed suicide squeeze bunt down the 1B line; it went 10' and died in the chalk as the O.K. White champs from the outlying area upset the favored big city all-stars.

The 1974 team was very experienced and accomplished a lot. When I was making team selections, I decided that Tom "Buckwheat" Pylman was likely a third-tier outfielder and probably would not be needed. When I told him something like that, he gave me a persuasive speech and told me I'd need his bat. Though he really got little playing time on this very strong team, he did happily drive in one game-winning run. Arg Loomans, who became Tom's father-in-law, was a longtime janitor and all-purpose guy at and for the school. With his sleeveless white T-shirts and a bunch of keys rattling at his hip, he knew how to pitch in. In the mid-70's he was a major force in moving the varsity diamond from the southwest corner to the northwest corner of the property on the 68th Street campus. Part of his legacy was his "argisms." Once he told the teachers about his pregnant niece who had "sisserean" surgery.

In one game with the temperature projected to be around 40 degrees, we played at Kimble Stadium with Brian Ellens on the bump. I believe we won 1-0 in a swiftly played game, but the temperature ended up at 36 degrees with snow falling lightly; it was the coldest baseball game I ever coached.

Early that season we weren't looking too sharp. We lost three of our first five; that included a big, bad loss to league power Wyoming Park after we made an incredible nine errors - a high school record possibly! We ended up, though, with a league title and a school high 23-5 season after beating East Grand Rapids High School in the regional opener before losing to a very mature looking Mt. Pleasant team in the regional final of the single elimination state playoffs.

After the 1974 graduation SCHS lost a talented group of multi-sport athletes; they relished being champs in both football and baseball for me: Bill Blacquiere (fullback/safety and 3B-man), Tom "Rook" Buist (linebacker/kicker and 2B-man), Brian Ellens (QB and pitcher), Jim "Miner" Meindertsma (split end and rightfielder), Pete "Moss" Mulder (defensive end and P/1B-man), and Tom "Toro" Roossien (rugged lineman and catcher). On top of that several of them were three-sport athletes. Roossien ended up working for an equipment company and Meindertsma in the grocery business while Mulder became a car salesman.

The **1976** team had one hardluck pitcher – southpaw throwing Billy "Berk" Berkenpas. In one game he struck out 15 Forest Hills Northern batters but lost a 1-0 game on an unearned run. But his .370 senior year batting average helped him to a Sailor best career batting average of .355. Post high school, "Berk" continued to play baseball and fastpitch all over the states and beyond; he prized his fastpitch trophy earned after a world championship game in Italy before his being inducted into the U.S. Fastpitch Hall of Fame in 2018. "Berk" carved a career out of the construction business. One of his colorful teammates was Chuck "Woody" Wustman, a spunky catcher who showed up for a game at Zeeland with a twinkle in his eye and chomping on a carrot; the Zeeland Chix had a really good SS whose nickname was "Rabbit." I learned later "Woody" became a C.P.A.

The **1978** ball club was a special Sailor squad and my last baseball team at SCHS. It was anchored by four seniors – rocket-armed C Greg "Red" Cook, P Walt Faber, 3B-man Randy VanHoven, and SS Mark "Cannon" Syswerda, and several really good juniors who made significant contributions. I wished I could've coached them the next year.

"Cannon" was first inserted into the starting line-up as a sophomore; as he recalls, he made five errors in his first start, a game in Zeeland, even though our team managed somehow to win 3-2. Later he told me that I'd assured him no matter what he was my SS of the future. As a senior the 5'6" mustachioed "Cannon" made some key plays in a final league game between us and Wyoming Park's Vikings. Both teams came into the game with 12-1 records. That day we used the fond formula of outstanding pitching and sure defense with clutch hitting to edge the Vikings. On a "web gem" play with two outs and no score but with a Viking baserunner at 3B, "Cannon" dove to his left to cut off a grounder headed for centerfield, got up, and fired a strike to 1B to kill a mid-game Viking threat. Later a base hit by "Cannon" to CF drove in the go-ahead run of the fantastic game at Kimble Stadium to give the Sailors another league championship. Walt Faber, our crafty southpaw ace, pitched the critical 2-1 win. Both VanHoven and Syswerda became accountants while Cook surveys for Exxel Engineering.

With his live arm Walt Faber had already thrown 93 miles per hour on a radar gun in the summer after his junior spring season, and he came into his senior season polished and confident with a blazing fastball and a sharp breaking curve ball. But as a sophomore Walt was a little wild on the mound. In his first nonleague game against Rogers he walked the bases full after 13 pitches and then threw one more ball; I took him out and told him to go to the bullpen and throw some strikes because he'd get more chances. My visit with him at the mound after eight ball pitches to start the game hadn't helped. After the game his short Dutch dad, chomping on a cigar, verbally slammed me in the parking lot; he said, "You have r-r-ruined Valter." Including a somewhat bumpy sophomore year, Walt's high school career pitching stats were an envious 18-6 win-loss record, a 1.63 era, 239 K/177 IP. It earned him a baseball ride to Western Michigan University for the Broncos for three years before three years as a pro in the Detroit Tigers' chain. His pro career ended after his third left elbow surgery in three years; later he turned to selling sporting goods.

In a conversation later with his teammate "Cannon" I learned a couple interesting items. During Florida spring training for pro ball in the Tigers' farm system, Walt Faber had just finished pitching against a couple of Red Sox legends – Jim Rice and Fred Lynn. As Walt was walking off the field, he was greeted by an older man who said, "Your ball really has movement; you have something special. If you keep healthy, you can have quite a career." That older man with the compliment was hall-of-famer Ted Williams, "the Splendid Splinter."

A couple of summers ago at age 57 "Cannon" played in Las Vegas for a 55-and-older slow pitch team that beat out 41 other teams to win the World Championship Tournament. As he approaches his 60s, he's still enjoying playing ball.

My reflections about my **football coaching** experiences at SCHS have some overlap with some of my baseball experiences. In the fall of '64, SCHS's inaugural football season, I as a rookie teacher volunteered to serve as an assistant to the junior varsity football coach Roger Brummel. After seven winless games and a 0-44 loss to Lee, Roger told me he was going to prepare for his upcoming junior varsity basketball season and asked me to coach the team the last week of the season. Somehow, our team won its final game of the season. The next year I was asked to be the junior varsity football team's head coach, and after five seasons of junior varsity coaching I was asked to follow John Bekkering to become the varsity football team's head coach.

I recall designing and installing a primary 5-3 defense with tall, rangy, and hardhitting Bruce Lubben at middle linebacker and with enthusiastic and energetic 130-pound Ricky DeMann, a rat terrier, as a guard-gap shooter from the nose guard position to free up "Bruiser" behind him. As a junior, Rickie's claim to fame was getting into a couple blowout games late to draw penalty flags for late hits. Once in a blocking drill "Bruiser" as a sophomore on my junior varsity team hit the dummy in front of my chest so hard I nearly bit off my tongue and landed on my tailbone; as a junior he broke his wrist, but wearing a cast cost him a game or two so he cut off the cast so he could play. A couple sure interceptions that he could not hang on to as a senior he could only blame on his floppy wrist. He certainly fulfilled Bear Bryant's wish for a football player: "to be agile, mobile, and hostile" (all with long i's). My requirement in those days that all the players run a 6 ½ minute mile seemed too much for "Bruiser" at first, but after a couple days he did it and got back to practicing with the team. I was relieved to have him on my team. He was indeed a punishing force as a 6'6", 215-pound middle linebacker. His working career has been in supply chain management while DeMann's work has evolved into an industrial repair ownership.

The coaches had trouble finding a perfect helmet fit for one player whose head was shaped like a Texas longhorn. That interesting character was Henry "Dixie" Faber (also known as "Tarzan"). Before his senior year his folks moved to Lynden, WA. Henry last before one week when he decided to motorcycle back to MI and find a place to stay for his final year. He found a hospitable family. On the gridiron he had some trouble with the designed defensive schemes; so we turned him loose to create havoc in his own way. He also took a course in judo and even applied a feet-to-the-chest hit on an unsuspecting opponent on a kick receiving team. His big grin has certainly etched a place in my memory.

The '72 fall we were 0-3 before hitting our stride as a ball club and ending up in second place in the 10-team league though we were the school with the smallest enrolment. A key lineman was our weakside guard, the cerebral Mike Vredevoogd; the year before he had hardly played, but as a senior he was a topnotch lineman; we ran one audible strictly behind his fine line leadership. Perhaps the most outstanding game played by a Sailor football team up to this point in its history was the 40-0 upset of the Godwin Wolverines; that wasn't what the local sportswriters had predicted. Pete "Moss" Mulder made a dramatic interception and ran it in for a touchdown off an errant Wolverine pitch play. Extremely rewarding was our 26-0 upset of the highly ranked Wyoming Park Vikings on our new joint field shared with Byron Center High School; Park had come in riding a 16-game winning streak; it's the only time I was hugged by cheerleaders. Our last loss that year was to a strong Zeeland Chix team that took advantage of our overly aggressive pursuit by wisely employing counter plays. Vredevoogd played at 190 pounds, but the University of Michigan scout that came to see me about him said he could only bulk up to 225 pounds, and he said the Wolverines needed linemen who weighed over 260 pounds if they were to beat Ohio State. Well, that was in the 1970's.

The '73 Sailor football team was outstanding. Its hallmarks were its solid defense keyed by Bill Blacquiere, a great safety and a rugged defensive end – Pete Mulder, and a very balanced and productive offense that averaged 125 yards a game from FB Bill Blacquiere – "Mr. Inside," 130 yards from junior tailback, Tom "Rooster" Elzinga – "Mr. Outside," and another 100 yards per game from QB Brian Ellens' passing, The day before our final league game with one-loss Wyoming Park at its homecoming we suffered a big loss – "Rooster" blew out his knee. Our undefeated team had a sudden disadvantage. That Friday night I had to move Blacquiere from FB to tailback in the second half, and with his "Powerhouse" runs and our play-action passes we gained a one-point lead, 22-21, with 80 seconds remaining. Before we kicked off, I told our kicker, Tom "Rook" Buist to kick the ball away from Mike Ball, later voted the league's Most Valuable Player and a shifty ball carrier. "Rook" kicked the ball off the helmet of one of the Vikings' front five, and it veered toward Ball, who got the ball and beat our crashing end down the left sidelines for an upsetting turnaround touchdown. Later when we viewed the game, we believe we saw Ball had stepped out of bounds on the chalk in his kick return. But the "zebras" didn't see it that way. So that fall the Vikings and Sailors were co-champs. Later "Rook" became a mortician after some training in Chicago, where one of his part-time jobs was serving the famed and sometimes "liquefied" baseball broadcaster and announcer Harry Caray as a personal driver. "Powerhouse" Blacquiere became a high school teacher and football coach before turning to administration for a lengthy stint after a satisfying college football career for the Hope Flying Dutchmen.

The next couple years were a bit disheartening as talent and sometimes desire seem to fall off; even the generally highly successful Sailor basketball coach Tom Dykema suffered through a 1-20 season during that stretch, but I still remember the 76-yard punt by Craig "Cruncher" Newhof, a fast and rambunctious linebacker who played college football first for Grand Rapids Junior College, where he got his grades up, and then at Central Michigan University even though his heart was first set on playing for the maize and blue Wolverines. The rugged "Cruncher" has built and remodeled more MacDonald's in Western Michigan than anyone else in his 40-year work span.

After leaving SCHS in the summer of '78, I especially treasure three memories connected to my years of coaching the Sailors. First, during my fifth fall in Washington (1983) on a Friday night I received a phone call from the seniors of my '73 SCHS football team. They were celebrating their high achievement of 10 years earlier with a reunion. The call came to me, as I now recall, deep in normal nighttime. Those guys stayed the night at a hotel after taking in a specially coached high school football game that pitted Hudsonville (Bill's team) vs. South Christian (Bob's team) in a kind of "Blacquiere Bowl." My former football players shared individually some fine late-night chats with me. It was very thoughtful and special of them.

Secondly when in 2001 I visited the town of Cutlerville, Michigan where SCHS is located, I called up some former ballplayers who might meet me for old times' sake; the local restaurant served breakfast to some 20 men, and we shared wonderful stories and laughter.

Thirdly, helping SC, the smallest school in the league with around 600 students, to earn 11 trophies in 11 years of baseball coaching and one league co-championship trophy in five years of football coaching has given me a solid source of satisfaction, but the relationships with a wonderful variety of athletes is what I treasure the most by far.

A Coach's Hope*

For long I doubt I'll have to wait
To see an artist carve the plate,
A hurler who with screwball pitch
Will make the batter's hands to itch,

Or one who will with blazing speed
Deliver strikes on batters' knees
Or one who will with clever hook
Leave batters standing, just to look.

Behind home plate the catcher's arm
Will freeze fast runners thinking harm;
Directing fielders, giving signs,
Top catchers cramp opposing nines.

Around the horn good gloves will stop
The low line drive, the nasty hop;
While fluid fielders shuffle low,
Big "stretch" at first will nab high throw.

Quick keystone pair turns double play
With pivot sharp and sure relay;
Hot corner fielder knocks down shots,
Reacting quick from many spots.

In pastures green three fielders roam
With high fly balls they feel at home;
By gliding back up to the fence,
They give the fans some real suspense.

Defensive baseball must be tough
Or pitching well is really rough;
Defensive fielders must show skill
Or pitching hopes are truly nil.

*I wrote this in iambic tetrameter (right before the 1978 league championship season)

Coaching Memories at LCHS (Lynden Christian High School) 1978-2006

Coming to the West Coast to teach in the fall of 1978 brought new experiences for a somewhat veteran coach. First of all, I agreed to coach the football boys of grades 7 and 8 at Lynden Christian Middle School. They seemed so inexperienced with only a couple of the boys really knowing how to hit; I called these young Lyncs my "Pablum People." Rich Appel and Jack "Lambert" Tiemersma were the first two to hit with reckless abandon on the gridiron. Today Rich Appel runs an efficient cheese business and Jack Tiermersma is a trucker. Our team consisted of very few sturdy young players, but we did manage to win half of our games. I recall playing one game against the powerful Lynden Lions on their home turf behind the Darigold plant. In those times teachers were asked to referee games even if they were not registered or trained by the state. With the young Lions sporting a healthy lead in the game, we tried a long developing play with flanker Kent De Boer, today a supervisor for Chevron, running a reverse from his wide receiver position. Surprisingly our execution was just deceptive enough for him to gain about 30 yards. Not surprisingly the umpire, Warren Pugh, threw a penalty flag. His reputation as a "homer" did seem to follow him as an "official." The referee, Jake Maberry, who was already the highly esteemed Lions' boys basketball coach whose license plate said "Mr. Lion," stated firmly, "That was no hold, Warren; pick up your flag!" That was our best play of the day. Years later Warren did become a registered high school football official, and I did referee a few games with him on my crew. Jake retired, as I recall, as the winningest basketball coach in the state of Washington to run his berry business and hunt and fish with cronies. In later years I did a lot of summertime painting on Jake's buildings at his country home. And we had some enjoyable conversations. Wonderfully, years later both the nominal believer and the Mormon of many years became believers.

Coaching baseball at any level at LC, where basketball has a long tradition as the lord of sports, had its challenges. Often dealing with the hangover after the four-day state basketball tournament and inclement weather while also competing with golf, track, and tennis then (soccer now) for players in a small high school required persistence.

The following spring I coached the high school's junior varsity baseball team, and I did that for a few years. Since the varsity team usually had to draw on quite a few sophomores and some freshmen in our high school which consisted of grades 9-12, building J.V. teams brought some real challenges. My first spring I had eight players left after the varsity team was formed. To have a J.V. team I called up the coaches in the county and asked them if I could lure some juniors in the halls of LC to have a J.V. team. I found three boys who agreed to play. One of those special persons was John VanderVeen. My first team played 10 games and lost all of them, but LC had a J.V. team to build with.

Early on I had a big, uncoordinated pitcher named Drew Roosma; to help him gradually gain some skill, polish, and confidence was a delight. Later as a varsity senior in '81 he played an awesome game by pitching a 14-inning shutout against the Blaine Borderites, and then he brought in the winning run himself with a big hit. Today he sells real estate in Eastern WA around which he annually spends a month on a mission in Africa.

I also recall a special moment for Duane "Dirt" Korthuis, a far-from-cocky freshman. On a cool, breezy day Duane got a chance to pinch hit with a runner on 2B. To calm his nerves, Duane scooped up some dirt and tossed it into his mouth; then he slammed a pitch into CF for a big RBI hit. Duane has had to deal with seizures in his life, but he's a model of humility and service as he works at Lynden High School assisting all the coaches and athletes with his first aid knowledge as the athletic trainer. That man has a killer smile, a family trait it seems.

In 1983 one of my J.V. teams played Ferndale. In a home game my players faced a promising and pretty powerful young pitcher named Darrin Nolan. Tad "Tater" VanderGriend, one of our best

9th graders and a kid with a hereditary fluid swing, will never forget his grand slam home run to left field off this pitcher who would later star in high school and college before playing pro ball in the Montreal Expo's farm system. Today Tad owns a lumber company that his grandpa and dad ran before him. During my J.V. coaching stint of 1979-1984, some of my J.V. players went on to play for Coach Bob Vander Haak, the LC varsity baseball coach and later a Hall-of-Fame girls' fastpitch coach for LC, and some "retired early."

For five seasons I served as the head varsity football coach at LCHS. Before a stronger weightlifting ethic was built, this coaching, too, was challenging. During the '78 fall, varsity team players would sometimes watch my "Pablum People" during an exciting drill. When head coach Fred Ypma, my very good neighbor, announced his retirement in the spring of '79, a large contingent of juniors surrounded my classroom desk one noon hour and declared I should be their coach the following fall. These guys were big on enthusiasm, and I gave in to their prodding. That first fall is clearest in my memory. The offensive lineman averaged about 160 pounds outside of the biggest lineman – Leroy "Wild One" Plagerman, who weighed 180 pounds; our tight end was Wendall "Rupe" (after Ruppert Jones, the Seattle M's centerfielder) Kaemingk, who was 145 pounds soaking wet. Behind Dan Kaemingk, the junior QB, was our fullback Don Top at a 165 pounds and the tailback Renier Eisses at 135. Going up against the Lions was a handful to say the least, but our guys like the spirited Mike "Swag" Schweigert and Jim Huleatt played with guts and guile. In the first meeting behind the Darigold plant the Lynden Lions' Kurt Langstraat, now a pastor, made a late pick that led to the winning touchdown for the home team. In the second meeting LC led till the Lions flooded our zone secondary with another late TD pass. In our first two games with the Lions we had two "just abouts" in the '79 season. Now Dan Kaemingk, my first LC varsity QB, has been a blessed long time LCMS teacher after playing football for Northwestern of Iowa; he is in his second stint as the very capable Lyncs head football coach. With the help of his 12 kids, Leroy is making a splash with robotic farming.

Prior to one practice session Dave "Tink" Tinklenberg, a smooth receiver, lost a contact lens in the end zone where we warmed up. For the entire practice we rotated two players at a time looking for where the lens had fallen. After practice "Swag" and I stayed with "Tink" to look a little longer. "Swag" announced his find; "Tink" ran over and said, "Let's see it." As "Swag" opened his hand, the lens sailed away in the wind. "Tink" said, "Let's get out of here!" Today "Tink" is a salesman for a plumbing company in Iowa.

During the '81 season Roger DeBoer, also an accomplished hitter for the baseball Lyncs during the springtime, kicked a field goal against the Blaine Borderites to give the Lyncs a sweet shutout victory. Later I recall our team winning at Mt. Baker when #88 Wade "Flash" VanderMeulen made a kickoff return of 88 yards for the game's only score; it held up when Jack Tiemersma tackled a Mountie running back just shy of the end zone to finish the game and preserve the shutout in Deming. Wade works in a gravel business today.

The **1983** team started its season with a bang. Undefeated after a few games, our team lost its senior QB, the confident and dynamic Jordan "JJ" Jansen, when he slipped and tore up a knee. Our junior tight end Kevin "Spanky" Kaemingk was moved to QB. The Lyncs played one very special game at Lynden that mid-season. Before school on that Friday morning I was in my classroom when I spotted something very unusual hanging from a rope in the grandstand; it was a big white dummy with the large numbers 666 painted in navy blue on it. Before the athletic director could take it down, I had my football players take a look at it. That night the boys in blue finished every tackle with a "Remember the dummy!" LC upset the Lions 27-9 to end a 7-game Lions' win streak in the rivalry. Our all-state tailback Tim "Veener" VanderVeen rambled for 207 yards behind the blocking of his strong line and fullback Tom "Badge" Bajema. Super pass catchers Tim "Zee" Zylstra and Mike VanWeerdhuizen led the aerial assault. "Badge" works in the sheet metal business while "Veener" is a dairy farmer today. Tim Z, also a basketball coach for LC, is an independent businessman while Mike has worked for the Weyerhouser Co. and Jordan is in banking business and still enjoys success playing adult baseball in the Seattle area.

Now I see the P.S. of those football players of yesteryear who were groomed at LC and then groomed others at LC. Jim Huleatt and John VanderVeen each have blessed LC with many years of coaching after playing football and baseball for LC. Jim served as a youth director before entering the real estate field while John works in agriculture. Mike Schweigert has served as a high school teacher, coach, and an administrator in Skagit County, now at Sedro Woolley. Dan "Special K" Kaemingk has notably led the LC football fortunes for many years while his brother Kevin has served for many years as a high school administrator. Roger DeBoer, already a Hall-of-Fame basketball coach, is presently the Lyncs head man on the hardwood. Dan and Roger have both led respective teams to state championships.

I shifted all my coaching energies toward LC baseball in the spring of **1985**. What I inherited was a somewhat limited stable. Only Kevin Kaemingk was a returning starter; earlier as a J.V. player I had taught him to switch hit. He had a modest .217 B.A. as a varsity junior. But as a senior he led the young Lyncs as our #3 batter by hitting .304 with 18 SB and playing LF. As a senior he put on one hitting reel highlight game. Learning to go with the pitch and facing a righthander, Kevin lashed an outside pitch for a base hit to LF, spanked a hit up the middle into CF, and finally on an inside pitch ripped a triple over the head of the Lynden Lions' big 1B-man Eric Peterson. We missed going to the playoffs as the third-place team in league as our captain Kaemingk was on a senior biology trip during our last game.

After a tight game at the Lynden diamond I was flattered to be asked by a couple of the Lion senior infielders if I would consider coaching for the Lions the next year as Rollie DeKoster was at the end of his lengthy coaching career. One highlight of the Lyncs'

'86 season was the suicide squeeze bunt of junior 1B-man Leonard "Smitty" Smit, our clean-up batter; perfectly executed, it scored Darren Johnson with the winning run to give Blaine's big righty Scott Baker his only defeat of the season.

After the '86 season I was asked to coach the county all-stars at the state feeder game in Bellingham. From that game I recall two things. All-star teammates of LC's Brian De Zeeuw couldn't believe how he dared to throw his breaking ball and change-up when behind in the count. And one member of our North team was three-sport athlete Doug Pedersen from Ferndale HS; as I learned in the dugout especially, he was so mature and easy to relate to as a young man. Today after a great college and pro career as a QB and years of assistant coaching in Green Bay and elsewhere, he presently serves the Philadelphia Eagles, the 2018 Super Bowl champs, as their head coach.

One **1987** game of that 14-win season stands out. Behind the strong pitching of senior Darren "DJ" Johnson, we led the Lynden Lions 2-1 going into the 7th at our yard. In the top of the 7th Lynden's catcher, Cory White, now the veteran head baseball coach for the Lynden Lions, belted a two-run homer to straightaway CF to give the Lions a 3-2 lead. But in the bottom of that last inning, Kevin "Spike" Stuit rolled a grounder through the wickets of the Lions' 2B-man, my son Dave drilled a game-tying triple to right-center, and then SS Brad "Gunner" Greenough drove a pitch that picked up some lime down the RF line to complete the exciting comeback with a walk-off win. As a senior, Dave had learned to go with the pitch; it helped him to 14 RBI to lead the league. This team's second place finish matched the finish of the '75 team. Today "Spike" Stuit is a trucker; "Gunner" directs a lot of action at an engineering firm while Dave is a college administrator and "Smitty" is an experienced insurance agent.

Don Murdzia has relished his very lengthy officiating career in the county's sports seasons. Before one baseball game he mentioned to us coaches he might do something unusual in the baseball game. At one point the best athlete on Ferndale's team, Darrin Nolan, easily stole 2B. However, Murdzia called him out. When Nolan vigorously protested, Murdzia tossed him. As Nolan steamed off the field, Murdzia shouted at him, "April fool!" and called Nolan back to 2B where he was indeed safe after all with a memorable April 1 stolen base.

The '88 team was propelled by four seniors – 1B-man Roy Clark, CF Kevin "Kiwi" Havert – son of our team's self-appointed chaplain, SS Brad Greenough, and C-P Barry "Bear" DeZeeuw. As a junior Clark had transferred from Lynden HS to LC. In his first 3 games he struck out each time as a pinch hitter, but his rip in game 4 left the Lions' 2B-man's glove stinging. From that point on Roy played RF or served as our productive DH. After graduating from Calvin College, he began a "Big Brothers" mission in the Grand Rapids area. For one annual banquet he secured Tony Dungy, the Super Bowl champion coach of the Colts, to come. Roy said it took 24 phone calls until he could get the Dungy commitment to speak at the banquet. Now in Florida, Roy, after a variety of working hats, is involved in the world of art displays and Kevin's a C.P.A. in MI.

After input from two former LC catchers who were alumni, Barry DeZeeuw as a freshman became my first catcher, part of a full four-year stretch as a baseball player. Later Scott "Scooter" Romjue ('96 grad) and Matti "Ma Ha" Haggren ('03 grad) were also deemed mature enough to handle varsity demands early on. Barry led the '88 team to its first district appearance in 12 years both as a catcher and pitcher, an extremely demanding double role. As the league MVP he batted .519 and played in the all-state games in Wenatchee. This team earned the first ever district championship for LC in baseball.

In one tight playoff game one verbal signal could've been disastrous. With Barry DeZeeuw dueling on the mound against Meridian's Chris Edmonds at Joe Martin Stadium in Bellingham, our three-hole hitter Brad Greenough was the 1B-runner when big lefty hitting Clark at clean-up ripped a two-out shot up the alley in the outfield. I was waving Greenough home before he reached 3B, but I saw Clark by 2B looking like he might try for 3B. I hollered, "Stop" with hands held high. Greenough was 2/3 the way home when he heard that verbal directive. He flew back to 3B to the stunned surprise of LC folks and fans at the game. I, too, was shocked. Our #5 hitter, Bill Diephuis, came up next and spanked a hard grounder at the Trojan's SS, but it was too hot to handle cleanly so Greenough scored the winning run in that 2-1 thriller which provided a teaching moment and some heavy relief for all the LC faithful. After high school both Brian and Barry DeZeeuw have worked in the construction business and Bill Diephuis is an engineer.

Tom "Zee" Zylstra had made some exciting defensive plays on defense as a junior, but in '89 he had a truly super individual season. His defense as a 2B-man was flawless (58 PO + A) as he handled every routine play in addition to several outstanding plays. In my 40 years of high school coaching he was my only 2B-man ever to achieve an error- free season besides shining with the bat; he hit for a .424 average on 25 hits. Tom manages a car parts store today.

Chad "Bovy" Bovenkamp really upped his pitching game as a senior. From throwing less than 50% strikes as a junior the year before to building a school record 1.28 e.r.a. senior season was a huge upgrade. In our final game of '90 we had our ace "Bovy" on the mound as we faced Granite Falls in a single elimination district game. But there were some concerning complications. We had lost our experienced senior catcher Kent Shelton to a knee injury half the way through the season. His replacement was junior Russ VandenBerg, who had done a very fine job behind the plate too. The morning of the district game I received a call from Russ's mother to inform me Russ was in bed with a temperature of 103 degrees. One of the things I had learned over the years was to prepare back-ups. I always tried to have three catchers who could serve in that critical position before the season got rolling. Four of our team's seniors had to be flown in from a tiring senior biology field trip. Trevor Veltkamp, our all-star 2B-man, arrived at the game and was very surprised to learn he was to be the catcher. He was more comfortable using his infield glove rather than a catcher's mitt to handle all of the movement of "Bovy" pitches. And there was a question about his wearing or not wearing a cup. The game was a tightly fought pitching contest. In the bottom of the 7th inning Granite Falls got the bases loaded with one out and the score tied at 1-1. Their batter got just enough of a "Bovy" breaking ball to tap it weakly a few feet down the 1B line. Trevor hustled to pick up the ball and touch home plate for out #2 and then fired to 1B. Since the ball was weakly hit, our first baseman had charged. The throw sailed about 5' over our covering second baseman by 1B. Our rightfielder Dwayne Lenssen was able to back up the throw, and he unleashed a rocket toward home as the 2B runner raced for home. However, his throw was far to the 3B-side of home plate and impossible for Trevor to catch. On one bounce the hard throw nailed the ondeck batter in the mid-section and he fell like a sack of potatoes as the winning run scampered home. Despite all the drama, no coach was ever prouder of his catcher and team that day than I was; Trev's work behind the plate was commendable; his only preparation had been two innings in a preseason game. Today "Bovy" works for the courts system in Seattle and Russ is a project manager for a flooring company while Trevor is an orthodontist. Trevor's dad Jack was a sophomore in '60 when the baseball Lyncs won a co-title in their first year of league play.

Arriving in '90 as juniors and transfers were a couple of LC's most explosive hitters ever and two of the most haunted by injury ever. Bob Hayden got off to a blazing start; with his gorgeous swing in league play he had seven hits in nine AB (8-11 for the season) till he slid into 3B at Mt. Baker HS with a triple only to break an ankle. Then in the off season he decided to play football. In his senior fall he was flipped on his shoulder and wrecked it enough that the following spring of '91 he could only throw about 90'. He was a rangy fly catcher so I put him in CF where he caught virtually everything in the air, and for relays my SS and 2B-man had to range far into the outfield to catch and relay his throws. One more thing happened to him; in a game against Lynden a Lion batter sent a drive to deep left-center where it rattled off the fence. However, LC had no warning track yet. Bob gave chase and banged into the fence, staggered around some before retrieving the ball and relaying it in. Dazed but undaunted, he soon discovered a tooth from his mouth was missing. After the fans and players of both sides emptied the stands to search for the missing tooth, it was discovered after 20 minutes just beyond the fence. The Lions rejoiced over the inside-the-park homer while Bob went straight to a dentist, had the tooth reinserted, and came back by the last inning when the game was out of reach. Since playing college baseball, Hayden has worked in the building trade and is helping an Indian tribe with its investments beyond casinos.

The other arrival in '90 was Jon VanderGriend. At his former high school he was used mainly for defense at 1B. After his first cuts during B.P. I was convinced I hadn't seen many more splendid swings. In an early season game Jon badly twisted his ankle and had to miss games for 10 days. But then he came on with a vengeance and hit a lofty .429 for that season. In football he was a 6'5 receiver with soft hands, and he led the county league in receptions his junior fall; he also was the friend of Bob Hayden who encouraged Bob to give football a try the next fall. As a senior Jon was throwing nearly 90 mph and had pitched a couple games before our spring trip tournament in Quincy. There he hurt his arm, and that was followed with mononucleosis for several weeks. He did come back to play some 1B and DH, but his season was certainly shortened by health concerns. With his sweet lefty stroke, "Vandy" still hit .420 in 50 AB and was intentionally walked a lot as was his cohort Hayden. The next year as a walk-on at the University of Washington he started a three-year span of awesome hitting there; his power hitting stats rivaled those set by former major leaguer Mike Blowers earlier. "Vandy" eventually signed with the Angels and played three years of pro ball before completing his engineering degree which led him into construction management.

Teammate Jeff Stremler, whose greatest outing was a 15-K no-no masterpiece against Cashmere, was kicked off his horse and suffered significant injuries shortly after he graduated from high school. A sign today by his house says, "Cribbage master." One other senior on that '91 team was Dan Teeter. From Canada, he was new to LC as a sophomore. He played a little J.V. ball, but as a junior he earned the right to be my DH and then as a senior my SS. He went on to Taylor University in Indiana where he played football and followed that up with teaching history and coaching football in Skagit County schools, and presently he is the head football coach at Lakewood HS in Smoky Point. One thing else about that '91 team: it was my only starting outfield in 40 years not to make an error; it consisted of Brian De Young (LF), Hayden (CF), and the powerfully armed Dwayne "the Rifle" Lenssen (RF).

One of the reasons those early '90's LC teams were stymied was lack of pitching depth. Another factor was play of Troy Slayton, a powerful player at Nooksack Valley HS. His senior year stats included a .613 BA on 19 hits besides 8 intentional walks and a 4-0 record on the bump with a 1.65 e.r.a. and 42 K in 17 IP. He was one of the best ever in the county, and later he became a fine power hitters' coach for the Lynden Lions. One year, I believe it was 1998, the Lions, featuring the Alexander twins and Matt Maberry, hit an amazing 30-some home runs under his tutelage.

On the **'92** team was junior Loren Terpstra. I first knew him as young neighbor boy. In middle school he hardly got to play, but as a lanky freshman he started to show promise. As a junior on a mediocre team he produced a 1.28 e.r.a. to tie "Bovy's" record. Some of his fellow juniors lacked focus during games. After the season was over, I asked "LT" to talk to his classmates, and then if they wanted to focus as seniors, they'd be welcomed back. Three of them hung up their cleats. Shortly after the season I received a long apologetic letter from one of the boys. But I have enjoyed a very positive relationship with all three, playing recreational basketball on a team with two of them. All three have become significant men as a teacher, banker, and cabinet maker/artist. Also on this team was Jason "Pokey" Blankers. For one major stat and a school record he collected eight RBI in a twin bill at Granite Falls one wonderfully productive day. Today he serves at a police academy.

Back for his senior season, "LT" with his prized number 24 on his back had become a great pitcher and teammate on a very successful team of much good talent. The '93 ball club won the first LC baseball league championship since 1969 when a bespeckled Hank Roorda led the way with his dominant pitching over two springs. The gritty '93 LC team won eight games by coming from behind. One newspaper reporter alluded to the earlier '69 championship with these words, "Man was about to set foot on the moon, the Mets were on their way to their first World Series' championship, and Lynden Christian won the Whatcom County League's baseball crown." A drought of 20 + years was over with the success of the '93 ball club.

Before a 0-1 loss, on an unearned run, in the district tournament, the meticulous and highly focused LT was 8-1 as a pitcher and the league's MVP. After the season "LT" was honored to pitch in the all-state game.

In 1993 the WCL was disbanded, and the next spring LC and many other teams became part of the North Cascades Conference. One of my joys with the formation of the new conference was coaching a few games against Mike Schweigert, my former ballplayer, as head coach of the Concrete HS team. Mitch "Pudge" Moorlag, a '93 junior and a good receiver, has served several springs for LC at the helm of the girls' fastpitch program while working in the dairy industry. Besides doing lots of assistant coaching at LC like Leonard Smit did, LT has worked largely within the hotel business. LT's new gig is serving at Seattle Seahawk games as the instant play technician on the sidelines.

The '94 squad of solid players garnered a second consecutive league title. The seniors were led by mature seniors - 1B-m and P Matt "Tiny" Kok and C Ryan "9-er" Diephuis. With his gun arm Ryan really restricted opposing baserunners, and he hit .410 besides. The southpaw arm of "Tiny" helped lead the mound corps, and his sweet lefty stroke produced 11 ebh and 23 RBI; he played in the all-state game after his productive senior season. This team's

16-win season was a new record for LC. Today Ryan works in the construction field while Matt is a financial advisor, mine in fact.

This team's 2B-man was Justin "Cruiser" Meenderinck, a fine defensive player and bunter, but one who knew the Mendoza line too well too long. A few days before our first district game, he asked me for special hitting help. I took him alone in the gym and pitched him several buckets of balls as he tried to hit the ball up the middle. For every batted ball that went through an open door behind me he earned a dollar. The extra practice proved to be fruitful as he went 3-6 to be our best hitter in the district doubleheader. And he finished HS baseball on a very positive note offensively. Now he is serving our country in strategic defense work.

"Beetle Bomb," the old gray school van, had its stories. As its driver for away games I used to see in my rearview mirror some string out the backside window. The string was the yarn of a former baseball which one senior was known to unwrap and dangle behind the van like a puppet show. That same senior once crawled into the aluminum box on top of the van; it must've been a little tight sharing the space there with the equipment, but after one game "Double Sticks" had a high ride from the ballpark to the McDonald's post-game meal.

To reach the final four at state in '94 we needed to defeat #2 rated Port Townsend and #1 rated Rochester. Port Townsend had an undefeated lefty named Jeff Wack. We decided to bunt him a lot. Mid-game after back-to-back suicide squeeze bunts by our dandy leadoff batter, Brent "Igniter" De Ruyter, and Lamont "Bossy" Bos right behind him, Wack was done, largely done in by our three nicely executed squeeze bunts. We scored nine runs in that regional opener, but we ran out of gas against the ace pitcher of Rochester in the regional final.

In '95 we rallied for 10 come-from-behinders to win a three-peat league championship. We were led in pitching by two juniors – Scott "Scooter" Romjue and Jess "Big Dog" Paulay. Jess threw a school record 67% strikes,and Scott was a very polished pitcher. By halfway through the season we had lost our starting catcher, Matt

Fleming. Reports from the east coast say "Flem" is highly educated now; already as a high schooler he was a heady conversationalist. To compete we needed another catcher behind the plate. "Igniter" DeRuyter had already been the all-league SS both as a sophomore and junior, but halfway through his senior season he volunteered to catch and "Bossy" moved from 3B to SS. This selfless team finally lost in the regionals to Stevenson by a score of 2-1 after my players persuaded me to pitch to their #3 batter with 1B open and a runner at 2B, but their hitter clutched up. That was my mistake. DeRuyter has long served LCHS as a teacher and its capable head soccer coach and Bos is as a correction officer.

After the '96 season we had to graduate Scott Romjue; his legacy in Lyncs baseball is truly impressive. He never missed a practice or a game in his 4-year high school career, and he was my #3 hitter in the batting order for every one of the 93 games. His career stats included a 19-9 record on the mound with 165 IP and 2690 pitches while collecting 100 base hits, scoring 77 runs, and driving in 56 more with his potent bat. The '96 team fell just one game short of winning a 4th consecutive league championship when the Meridian Trojans started to build some championship runs.

But Scott's and the team's saddest game was the last one. In the bottom of the 7th and final inning, Scott was pitching a shutout and no-hitter, and Lakewood had a runner on 1B with 0 outs. Their lanky 1B-man failed in his two attempts to lay down a sacrifice bunt but then got the first hit of the game for the Cougars by blooping the next pitch into short RF. The 1B-runner made it to 3B. With runners on first and third we intentionally walked the next batter to set up force outs. However, the next pitch was a low outside fastball which our sophomore catcher tried to shift to his right to catch without backhanding his mitt; the ball just missed his mitt. The 3B-runner got a bit of a late start but then raced for home. Our catcher raced to the backstop to retrieve the ball, and he got it in time to throw out the runner at home except his right foot slipped so he couldn't throw the ball. It had rained that day, and that play pulled the reins on the season. To say it was a defeat that was disheartening would be a large understatement. Today Scott Romjue is a regional manager for Old Navy and other stores in Hawaii while Jess Paulay works for a sprinking business.

On a side note, an amazing run of stats gals are a part of the baseball history at LC. These young ladies have blessed me particularly and LC teams for many years. A player on the 1960 LC baseball team was a young sophomore, Bob Terpstra. He and his wife Nella raised some wonderful kids. The 1996 season was the last season of a Terpstra stat gal; Carleen, Sheri, Kristi, and Kara each had faithfully served for many seasons as stat gals; they, of course, claimed LT as their good brother.

Some uncommon things came from the '97 team. One of the captains was a hard hitting and very rangy outfielder - Tim "the Tool Man" VanderMey. He finished off the Meridian Trojans with a walk-off home run in the season opener. Till 2017 he owned the school record for 11 HBP. On the bench was his girlfriend Danya Vander Veen, who was a creative and exacting stat gal as I ever had. After high school Tim and Danya were married in front of a fire truck as Tim made a career of being a fireman. Maybe he should have been a relief pitcher; he might've been the "fireman" of the league. I believe the '97 team was the only sport team in LC history to put on a chapel at school, and the songs the team sang on the bus were very uplifting.

The sophomore 1B-man on that team was Nick "House" Scholten. He was quick to learn from and apply everything his coaches gave him; one assistant coach said after the first practice, "the big kid in the gray sweatshirt listens to everything I say." Physically he stood out at 6'5 and 300 pounds. As a freshman on the J.V. team the year before he hit .250. But as a sophomore on the varsity he hit an impressive .457 with his keen and disciplined eye that produced a 66% OB despite protecting a big strike zone. What is impressive is how svelte Nick looks today after shedding some of his football career weight after college. He sells insurance today in Iowa.

The '98 squad was strong, with a very veteran presence.

Rebounding from a bout with mononucleosis the year before, Kevin "Dr. K" Roosma had a magical season on the mound as he threw three no-hitters with lots of strikeouts to rugged catcher Josh Parsons. I recall a regional game played in Bothell on Ingemoor's high school carpet. There we faced Charles Wright with its the University of WA commit, southpaw Zach Daniels with his 90-mph fastball and perfect 10-0 record. Our outstanding lead-off batter, CF/P Greg "Bulldog" Dykstra (with 60% OB; once he had a 5-hit game), led off with a walk; with only a one-way lead he forced a balk. Our always impeccably dressed 2B-man, Kelby Postma, ripped a double to LF, and our #3 batter, SS Scott "Watts" Van Andel, laced a triple over 1B and into the RF corner to give us a shockingly quick lead. After a 33-pitch first inning, Zach Daniels was dazed. After five innings the game was over; the score was LC 10, Charles Wright 0 as "Dr. K" shut them out with his third no-no. After the game was over, our kids had to sweep up all the seeds off the carpet by our dugout.

In our next game we played against Toledo on the University of Washington's carpet. Mid-game in a 3-3 tie, Toledo had a 3B-runner, and we guessed the squeeze bunt was coming; our pitcher threw a pitch high and away, but as the infielders charged, somehow the batter could just reach the ball and popped the pitch over our charging 1B-man Scholten's head, and the ball that fell for a base hit was so high that our agile pitcher almost got over and under it. That run and a couple more later for Toledo sent a very, very good LC team packing after a 17-win season, a highwater mark for the Lyncs. This may have been my most cerebral team as it was led by some straight A students who used van trips for studying. After high school Greg played football for Western Washington U and Scott added his name to his father Doug's for baseball records at Dordt College. For work Kelby has a construction crew, Kevin is in lawn care, Scott in marketing, Greg in engineering that has led to being an operations' manager, and Josh Parsons, the sterling catcher on that team, in ministry and education work after years with Youth with a Mission. It's worthy to note that Greg's father

Glenn was an outstanding Lyncs' ballplayer in the mid-'70's, and he was a driving, passing, and shooting force in the unique "Six Iron Lyncs" story of an unusual trip to the 1976 state basketball championship for LC.

One of the above '98 seniors chose to take to the junior-senior banquet a classmate who was not highly esteemed and gave that lad a shot in the arm; he was the first fetal alcohol student I taught. One of these same seniors was in the third or fourth grade and a captain for playing softball during a recess. When one kid was left unchosen and the other captain did not want him, the kind captain said, "We'll take you. And where would you like to play?"

Providing incentives to the players are a part of coaching. In earlier years at SCHS I wore a green sport coat every day after the baseball Sailors had won a game. Later I would not shave my upper lip till we lost and broke a winning streak. A couple times we got to 12 or 13-game winning streaks as I recall. At LCHS sometime in the '90's, I started to reward the players with a "slucky" after a win in Deming at Mt. Baker HS. The origin of "slucky" was actually a Dutch word "slokkie" that I heard of when my grandparents served some kind of fermented drink when I was a boy. The "slucky" for my players was a Coke or Pepsi after beating the Mountaineers. Greg Dykstra liked to ask during the school day if we were going to stop for a "slucky" if we won that day. When Daniel Vander Kooi was a senior, Mt. Baker's game at our park was postponed and became part of a doubleheader at their school. Daniel wondered if we had to win both of those games for a "slucky;" I said yes. That day we had a special "slucky" in Deming country. Maybe I should have promised a reward for other away games as our record at Mt. Baker was the best against any one team over the years.

One player made his mark in the '99 season. Besides hitting several home runs, senior 1B-man Nick Scholten crushed a foul ball that screamed above the 5' fence and through the 1' opening in the front of the 3B dugout and left a dent showing the imprint of the ball's laces into the back wall of the dugout. Fortunately nobody was hurt, but the next season the A.D. insisted that the fence be a foot higher.

The '00 Lyncs played very good defense. Their team fielding average was .939. Righty Landon "Lando" VanDyk threw hard as the team's workhorse. In one game he fanned 16. In another game he creatively used Super Glue to overcome a blister problem to keep pitching. In one unique game at Mt. Baker our #2 batter, DH Aaron "Beeker" Visbeek, had four successfully executed bunts including a squeeze. And at Sultan, captain Mark "Posty" Postma was hit by a pitch three times, and the last time when he got to 1B, the pitcher tried to pick him off but hit him again. After the game the Sultan Turks' coach gave "Posty" the "Pepsi" award as the best player of the game. Normally their coach gave it to one of their players. Once an engineer, VanDyk has become a dairyman and Postma a campus policeman for the University of Washington while Visbeek has transitioned from being an electrical engineer to a patent attorney.

2001 was a glory-filled season for the Seattle Mariners and Ichiro, who won 116 games, and for the LC Lyncs, who won 22 and finished 3rd at state, LC's highest finish yet after 60 years of high school baseball. As one coach said, "Those guys were gamers." Winning 14 of 16 in April games anchored the season. This squad was capably led by tri-captains Mike Ruble, Trenton "T-Dog" DeBoer, and Daniel VanderKooi. Just a year earlier "T-Dog" hit .083 on three base knocks; as a great CF/lead-off batter as a senior he hit .311 on 23 hits, with 21 SB, and 32 runs scored. Similarly, rugged catcher Ruble as a junior hit .115, but as a senior clean-up batter he hit .389 besides serving as an excellent catcher. VanderKooi, once an apple-cheeked and determined freshman, put together an extraordinary senior season as he went 10-0 on the mound and picked up 41 RBI with his .400 BA and 13 ebh with his bat – a majestic pitching and big offense combo. Mike set a record with 185 PO. Daniel still holds the LC school record with his T.O. A. (total offensive average) of 1.83; better than just looking at a player's B.A. in a short season, I used the TOA calculation which includes one plus point for every single, extra base hit, walk, HBP, getting on by an error or interference with two plus points for each sacrifice or RBI but 1 minus for every strikeout or POB; always the goal for a player was to average at least one good thing per an AB to be productive. Daniel, like Mark Postma before, also had excellent base-running instincts. Combining pitching and offense stats, Daniel had the best single season in my coaching career. Besides running an insurance business, the enterprising VanderKooi is presently directing the fortunes of LC varsity baseball. Like Tim Bouma of the '86 team, teammate Kyle Tjoelker, who was tough to strike out, proved to be a sports trivia expert as we rode the van for away games. Junior outfielder Josh Visser had the best AB for a run-and-hit I ever saw. It was in a game at Concrete HS, and the pitch he hit was about a foot above the bill of his helmet; he laced a single into left-center to move our 1B-runner to 3B.

The journey of the **'02** team was interesting though tested by suspensions and health issues. This team was led by LF Josh Visser and SS Clint "Ozzie" Bosman, the captains. Josh was full of enthusiasm and Clint, who still holds school records for assists for LC shortstops and sacrifices, agreed to do his "Ozzie" flips if we won the state championship. In a district game in Mt. Vernon Josh made a great leaping two-out catch at the LF wall to rob a South Whidbey Falcon of an extra base hit and preserve a one-run win; later that day, in the district championship game against Nooksack he drove in the winning run with a big hit.

Our biggest, most thrilling game came against 6'6" K.C. Jones and his Eatonville teammates in the regionals. Jones, like Zach Daniels and Jeff Wack earlier, reportedly threw in the 90's on the gun. So, as earlier, we prepared to face that kind of speed by having close-up batting practice pitches and the Jugs machine in the cage turned up high as our players worked to make contact by hitting the ball to the opposite field. Sure enough, the field monitor put up the speed of each pitch, and Jones was in the low 90's. Our pitcher was junior Mark "Ma Ho" Holleman, whose season's stats were an envious 9-1 record with a 1.17 e.r.a.; his high speed was 86. Matti

"Ma Ha" Haggren led off the game with a single to RF, and "Ozzie" in the two-hole did the same which led to a run. Soon we were in a pitching battle.

In the bottom of the 7th inning Eatonville filled the bases with 0 outs and its four, five, and six batters coming up. There were some lumps in Lyncs' throats. But not in the determined Holleman's; he dramatically struck out three batters in a row to force extra innings. In the top of the 9th Ryan Petronella's hit keyed a two-run rally that led to a 4-2 triumph.

Sorry to say, but we must've shot our wad in the regional opener because a floodgate of LC errors and opponent hits in the game right after sent us home. Imagine catching what was probably the longest regional doubleheader in LC's baseball history in the sweltering heat; that's what Nate Bosman admirably did that day. Some have said the toughest challenge in high school athletics is the Saturday of the regional tournament for baseball. Win two and go to state as one of the final four; lose one earlier or later and your season is over. Now "Ozzie" is a videographer while Josh works for a construction company.

One coach had thought Josh would not have the maturity to play varsity ball for me, but when he was a senior, I recall one situation during practice. That day I had no assistant coach to help direct the other skill stations while I threw BP. Josh was feeding me balls to pitch. He noted a couple of younger players on the hillside behind the 3B dugout were not practicing at their stations as they should and mentioned it to me. I asked him what we should do about it. He said for me to pull the two youngsters over and have them run the facility's fence line. I followed Josh's suggestion, and the youngsters practiced with focus after that. Josh turned out to be a true delight to coach.

The '03 ball club was another strong LC team, anchored by nine seniors. The captains were "Ma Ha," "Ma Ho," and sturdy catcher Nathan "Nate" Bosman. Our lead-off batter and 3B-man was Kevin Kooy; the year before he became our "McLemore," like the Seattle Mariners' ultimate utility man, capably playing a variety of defensive positions.

As a senior he was extremely productive with his .373 BA on 28 hits, 65% OB, 14 SB, and 33 RS. He may be the best lead-off batter I have ever coached for one season. All this he achieved after a pretty severe football knee injury the previous fall. Today "Ma Ha" is a commercial fisherman, and "Ma Ho" is a sales rep for software. Kevin Kooy is a local businessman while "Nate" sells insurance besides coaching at LC.

Two things stand out in my memory for the '04 team. CF Ryan "Bogie" Bogaards had hit .338 in 66 AB as a junior. I hoped he'd be even better as a senior. He was. He hit .339 and with only two "questionable" strikeouts as he played superbly though plagued by an aching hip both years. Sophomore Zach De Boer put together three unusual things in one game against Concrete: as a batter he laid down an excellent suicide squeeze bunt; as a pitcher he both started the game on the mound and finished it there returning to earn the save. Zach is a banker today while "Bogie" works in the hay business.

The '05 LC team I coached led me to do some head-scratching. Our last game was at home against Mt. Baker. In the bottom of the last inning with runners at 3B and 2B, one out, and trailing by a run, our big strong senior batter lined a shot to medium LF; the LF-er caught it by his ankles for out #2. What looked like a game-winning two-out, two-run walk-off base hit turned into a game-ending DP when our 2B-runner, another senior, was doubled off 2B. I really felt bad for Brent "V-dub" Van Weerdhuizen, who had pitched his heart out for us. Today he serves many of the community out of his machine shop. When the team ended up with a 0-17 record and a 6.10 e.r.a. and a .869 fielding average, I felt like I could not provide the necessary inspiration to help improve those players. I lost sleep over it and decided it was time for me to move on. Darren Johnson, who played CF and pitched well for LC from '85-'87, was moved up from J.V. head coach to varsity head coach the next year. Over the years DJ has willingly served LC in a variety of coaching positions around his work as a real estate agent. Juan Hernandez was another capable assistant who served a good stretch as a noteworthy pitching coach.

Over the years I tried lots of ways to motivate my players. Sometimes I didn't shave my upper lip till a winning streak was over. In memory of my three base hit game off a Kalamazoo pitcher in college, I rewarded my high school players with a check (starting with $5 first and ending with $13 my last years) if they got a base hit off the pitcher's glove or body. It helped to make hitting the ball up the middle a goal unless the pitch was a little inside or outside. Of course, errors by the pitcher did not count.

For years I prepared a "Monday Missive;" these missives included copies of newspaper clippings, stats, scheduling, etc. - a tool for communication with my players and their parents. Each season I made a post-season booklet with a recap and stats. My last one included some lessons I hoped the players could learn from playing high school baseball: 1.)Things are never as good or bad as they seem; 2.)Taking responsibility for one's actions is important in life; 3.)Some things have to be done even if they are not fun. Added was my favorite verse, Phil. 4:13: "I can do everything through him who gives me strength." (NIV) After 40 years of coaching high school baseball, a humbling game, I had worn the navy blue and white proudly over 800 games for two schools. I bled blue just like the Dodgers' Tommy Lasorda. Today I try to serve as the LC's baseball link to the past and as an encourager in the present. Gradually I had to learn to appreciate the process and not just the product or final score. I am very thankful for a long list of capable and helpful assistant coaches for their time and talent investments. I'm glad I never got booted out of a game by a troubled ump; I really came close once, by an uptight rookie ump at Nooksack. The relationships with players and seeing boys become men were among the greatest rewards in coaching; that is far more important than being an athlete or coach and having a career in the work world.

It is interesting to note that on the 1960 champion Lyncs team of long ago were several players whose sons later played on teams of LC that I coached. Already mentioned were then sophomores Bob Terpstra and Jack Veltkamp, but the batting order's #2, 3, 4, and 5 hitters, all seniors in '60, had sons that played for me: my infielder son Dave, Sherm Polinder's son Jeff, Harold Terpstra's son Grant, and Arlen De Young's son Brian – these sons were all good outfielders. Jeff is a hoof trimmer, Grant is a Navy Seal, and Brian is in construction; building must be in the De Young genes.

What followed my 42-year teaching career were some big blessings. At age 64 I retired from teaching. In the 2006 summer I was privileged to help coach the Washington state all-star baseball team to victories over Idaho and Oregon. That year I continued an enjoyable stint of playing in an adult league baseball league from age 60 through age 71; I managed to hit for a .294 average my first 10 years before tasting the Mendoza line the last two years and getting thrown out at 1B after what looked like a wonderful base knock to RF. My arm and wheels were falling off. Spending a couple weeks since 2007, my first retirement year, in AZ's "Valley of the Sun" to watch Mariner and Dodger spring training games with my wife Jeannie has been an annual rite for 13 March springs.

As a retiring teacher in June of 2006 I was asked to deliver the graduation address. After it the school administrators brought me a surprise: a three-ring binder full of information about Cooperstown and major league baseball's Hall of Fame and money for me to travel there. After being inducted into the Washington State High School Baseball Coaches' Hall of Fame in the fall of '06, my wife and I truly enjoyed being part of the biggest crowd ever (82,000) in Cooperstown, New York as Tony Gwynn and Cal Ripken, Jr., both career long one-franchise-only players, were inducted into major league baseball's Hall of Fame. Later attending the annual state coaches' Hall of Fame banquet at the Mariners' T-Mobile Park with Rollie DeKoster of Lynden, Blaine's Gary Clausen, and Meridian's Dan Hollod brought special recollections.

In 2015 I fulfilled a bucket list item. A high school teammate of mine, Arlen DeYoung, joined me in attending a Dodger fantasy camp for a week of baseball under the AZ sun. Rubbing shoulders with several players like Tommy Davis, Rick Monday, and more of the Dodgers' 1981 World Series championship team members was lots of fun. Also helping to bring together the 1960 LCHS baseball team for its first reunion, after 57 years, in the summer of 2017, was a blessing as 12 of the living 14 could make it a fine time to share stories of the past.

I wish I could've recalled more stories so that every former ball player could've been included. As it did for me, playing high school ball for many kids has added something special to their high school experience. One thing is sure: playing sports at higher levels is really relative. I wonder if many of my fine athletes would be in the starting line-up for a high school with an enrolment of 4,000 students. In my stories I have chosen not to focus on setbacks and or negative experiences but on the positive memories. Being gifted to be an athlete is something to be thankful for. Serving faithfully in the work force for one's career is very important. But being a godly man in all ventures of family life, career, and beyond is vastly more important.

Checking up on many of my former ballplayers has been rewarding when I was able to reach them and learn what they are doing now. But it seems as they were blessed as athletes, they are now blessing others as family members, church members, community members, and some even as ball players yet beyond their life's work. I wish I could have connected with all of them. I hardly can imagine that some of my Sailor ballplayers of yesteryear are already knocking on the door of retirement. They are getting older! But aren't we all?

As I have rounded 3B and am heading toward home in my life's journey, I am abundantly grateful for all the blessings that God has lavished on me – wonderful parents, health, opportunities with teaching, playing, and coaching, an understanding wife Jeannie and family, and so many wonderful players and coaches to be involved in sports with. I'm ready for home, but I hope it does take a little while before I get there. It will be quite a homecoming, no doubt, and I'll be handed a robe better than any uniform I ever wore. PTL!

1944

Father + son

1944

1943

20 mos

1956

8th grade graduation

Me at 2 with Dad, me at 20 mos., my 8th grad. in 56.

1960

1963-1964

dating

LCHS graduation

1964

GRJC catcher waits to no avail for baseball that senior John Roseboom has slammed over the outfield fence for a home run.

College baseball

My HS grad. in '60, dating Jeannie in '63, my college grand slam in baseball in '64.

Wedding
1965

Dave 10, Paul 8, Kara 5

Our wedding in '64 and our 3 little kids in '76 approximately.

SCHS '72

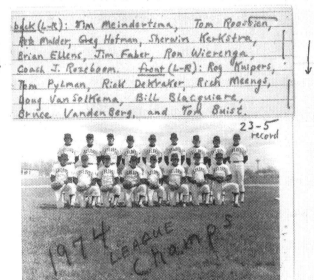

SCHS teams: '72 football and '74 baseball.

Ric, Ger, Ida, John
Mom + Dad

My parents and siblings in '95.

ELIZABETH ROZEBOOM

GEORGE ROZEBOOM

+

Obits' folder pictures of Mom '07 and Dad '12.

1999 LYNCS

back row (L-R): Coach Loren Terpstra, Evan Marcus (jr.), Tyler Coston (sr.), Mark Postma (jr.), Nick Scholten (sr.), Jeff Shaw (jr.), Landon Van Dyk (jr.), Jason Matter (jr.), Coach John Rozeboom

front row (L-R): Aaron Visbeek (jr.), Daniel Vander Kooi (so.), Lee Van Groningen (jr.), Kyle Van Andel (so.), Kevin Dykman (jr.), Mike Ruble (so.)

in middle front: Lisa De Haan and Sarah Haggren (stat gals)

missing: Coach Leonard Smit and Coach Mike Haggren

LCHS's '99 baseball team.

144

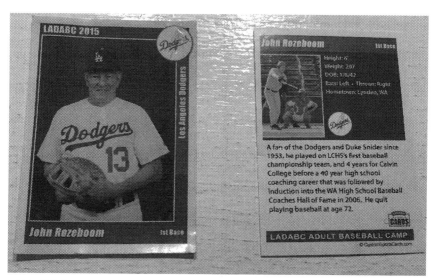

My '15 fantasy camp picture with the front and the back of the card.

2019 Spring Training

Spring training with Jeannie in '19.

Total family at Scottsdale reunion in '19.

Jeannie and I with the grands in Scottsdale '19.

Index

6   Nikita Khrushchev

7   Archie Walker

8   John Arlyn Rozeboom, Billy Rozeboom, Ron Schaap, Lou Ann Schaap and Gene Kuiper, Cliff Christians, Aud and John Fritz Schaap, and Dave Schelhaas

9   Bill Verwolf

10 Pete Bosman, Rhonda VanderPol, Dave Verwolf, Elton Visser, Alan Groen, Jay DeVries, Herb Advocaat, and Ray Bajema

12 Kenny Bosman, Alice Likkel, Clarence Schaart, Mr. Gerrit Likkel, Jackie VanDiest, Hattie Rensinbrink, Dena VanderStoep, Joe Levac, Sharon Smith, Anton Mellema, Dick Mellema, Billy Verwolf, Merv Dykstra, Myron Alsum, Denny Scheffer, and Georgia Postma

14 Rita Rozeboom (Fey), Jackie Robinson, Buster Mathis

15 Cliff Bajema, J.K. VanBaalen, John Fakkema, Garris Timmer, Bob Oordt, Gordy Buys, Peter Eldersveld, Vin Scully, wife Jeannie, Art Hommes, Jim Wynstra, Donna Veltkamp, Merle Meeter, Gerry Rozeboom, and Mark VanderArk

16 Elgin Baylor, Paul Hornung, Ken Griffey, jr., and Ben Pekelder

17 Rick Holleman, Ricky Mouw, and son Dave Rozeboom

19 Jim VanderMay, Ben Boxum, Larry Hagan, and Al Stremler

20 Ken Terpstra, Virg Vis, Paul Beezhold, Gord Hassing, Denny Brasser, Jim Harkema, Dave Wagner, Tom Smedes, Art Frens, Howard Rienstra, John H. Bratt, Steve VanderWeele, Don Wilson, Barney Steen, and Gay Digerness

21   Clarence and Mary DeJong, Gerrit and Gerdena (Scholten) DeJong, Art (and Eleanor) DeJong, Kathleen DeJong (and Jerry Andrews), Phyllis DeJong (and Jerry Witsken), Walter Ackerman, Sr., and Larry Bouma

22   Ted VanderMey, Lee VanderArk, Sherm Polinder, Ken Haak, Harry Sturrmans, Cecil Stuurmans, Harold Terpstra, Ken Faber, Matt Kok, John VanderMolen, Don Vroon, Ralph Honderd, Jerry Terpsma, Rich Hofman, Dan Lagastee, Phil VanSlooten, Tommy Lasorda, and Dusty Baker

23   Bill Hendricks, Dick Woudstra, Don and Alyce Boender, Henry Baron, Ed Start, Brian Diemer, Jacki VanderMolen, Bob Blacquiere, Don and Marcia Steeby, Harlan Kredit, Arv Blankers, Marv VanderPol, Rob Visser, Jordan Roorda, Rafael Siebenscheim, Prim Hangladoram, Brandon Rutledge, Judd Rinsema, Ed Compaan, Bill Brouwer, Don Kok, Keith Lambert, Gord DeYoung, and John Verstraete

24   Paul Hafford, Cory Bergman, and Monte Walton

25   Ned Betts, Jeff Morrison, Steve Chapman, Jacob Ferry

26   Ben DeRegt, Hanky DeGroot, and Casey DeGroot

28   John M. and Valerie VanderMolen, Jonathan Houghten, Liz Engelhard and Becky, Bethany, and Melissa, Eric Rozeboom, Sharon VanBeek and Tonya (Smith) and Leesha, and Loren Rozeboom

29   Deena Shriver and Drew, Dani, Desi, and Dakota, Paul and Sue (Jager) Rozeboom and Liesl and Annemarie, and Kara Rozeboom and Josh Gillanders and Kenzie and Caden

30   Joey Cora and Crissy Haden

31 Curt Brink, Orv and Keith VanderGriend, Joel Hoekema, and Shane and Cole Bajema

32 Harry and Phyllis Kuiper, Les Kuiper, and Jon Young

33 Dave Henderson, Arlen DeYoung, Steve Yeager, Rick Monday, Bill Russell, Tommy Davis

36 Walt Faber, Jon VanderGriend, John Meindertsma, Paul Theule, Garry Ringnalda, Paul Griffeth, Billy VanderHaar, Marv Hofman, Jerry Syswerda, Jim Czanko, Doug Kramer, Doug Tjaaties, Gord Oeverman, Tom Ellens, Dick Norden, Larry Kerstetter, Larry Zinger, Tom Moore, Brian Ellens, David Coates , Bill Blacquiere, Tom Pylman, Arg Loomans, Tom Buist, Jim Meindertsma, Pete Mulder, Tom Roossien, Billy Berkenpas, Chuck Wustman, Greg Cook, Randy VanHoven, Mark Syswerda, Jim Rice, Fred Lynn, Ted Williams, Roger Brummel, Bruce Lubben, Ricky DeMann, Henry Faber, Mike Vredevoogd, Tom Elzinga, Mike Ball, Harry Caray, Tom Dykema, Craig Newhof, Rich Appel, Jack Tiemersma, Kent DeBoer, Warren Pugh, Jake Maberry, John VanderVeen, Drew Roosma, Duane Korthuis, Darrin Nolan, Tad VanderGriend, Bob VanderHaak, Fred Ypma, Leroy Plagerman, Wendall Kaemingk, Dan Kaemingk, Don Top, Renier Eisses, Mike Schweigert, Jim Huleatt, Kurt Langstraat, Dave Tinklenberg, Wade VanderMeulen, Jordan Jansen, Kevin Kaemingk, Tim VanderVeen, Tom Bajema, Mike VanWeerdhuizen, Tim Zylstra, Eric Peterson, Rollie DeKoster, Leonard Smit, Darren Johnson, Scott Baker, Brian DeZeeuw, Doug Pedersen, Cory White, Kevin Stuit, Brad Greenough, Don Murdzia, Roy Clark, Kevin Havert, Barry DeZeeuw, Tony Dungy, Scott Romjue, Matti Haggren, Chris Edmonds, Bill Diephuis, Tom Zylstra, Chad Bovenkamp, Kent Shelton, Russ VandenBerg, Trevor Veltkamp, Dwayne Lenssen, Bob Hayden, Mike Blowers, Jeff Stremler, Dan

Teeter, Brian DeYoung, Troy Slayton, the Alexander twins – Dominic and Dante, Matt Maberry, Loren Terpstra, Jason Blankers, Hank Roorda, Mitch Moorlag, Matt ("Tiny") Kok, Ryan Diephuis, Justin Meenderinck, Jeff Wack, Brent DeRuyter, Lamond Bos, Jess Paulay, Matt Fleming, Bob and Nella Terpstra and Carleen, Sheri, Kristi, and Kara, Tim VanderMey, Danya VanderVeen, Nick Scholten, Kevin Roosma, Josh Parsons, Zach Daniels, Greg Dykstra, Kelby Postma, Scott VanAndel, Glenn Dykstra, Daniel VanderKooi, Landon VanDyk, Aaron Visbeek, Mark Postma, Ichiro Suzuki, Mike Ruble, Trenton DeBoer, Tim Bouma, Kyle Tjoelker, Josh Visser, Clint Bosman, K.C. Jones, Mark Holleman, Ryan Petronella, Nate Bosman, Kevin Kooy, Ryan Bogaards, Zach DeBoer, Brent VanWeerdhuizen, Juan Hernandez, Jeff Polinder, Grant Terpstra, Tony Gwynn, Cal Ripken, jr., Gary Clausen, and Dan Hollod.

Printed in the United States
By Bookmasters